D1709674

TIGER
BATTALION
507

TIGER
BATTALION
507

Edited by

HELMUT SCHNEIDER

Foreword by

Robert Forczyk

Translated by

Geoffrey Brooks

Greenhill Books

Tiger Battalion 507
This English-language edition
first published in 2020 by
Greenhill Books,
c/o Pen & Sword Books Ltd,
47 Church Street, Barnsley,
S. Yorkshire, S70 2AS

www.greenhillbooks.com
contact@greenhillbooks.com

ISBN: 978–1–78438–496–8

Publishing History
First published in German in 2016 as
Erinnerungen an das Panzerregiment 4 und die Tigerabteilung 507
by Fleschig Verlag.
This is the first English-language edition
and includes a new foreword by Robert Forczyk.

Original text © Verlagshaus Würzburg GmbH & Co, KG, Würzburg
Fleschig Verlag, 2016
Robert Forczyk foreword © Greenhill Books, 2020
Translation by Geoffrey Brooks © Greenhill Books, 2020

The right of Helmut Schneider to be identified as editor of this work
has been asserted in accordance with Section 77 of the
Copyrights Designs and Patents Act 1988.

CIP data records for this title are available from the British Library

Designed and typeset by Donald Sommerville

Printed and bound by CPI Group (UK) Ltd, Croydon CR0 4YY

Typeset in 11/14.5 pt Adobe Caslon Pro

The publishers would like to thank the following individuals and organisations for supplying
many of the photographs used in this book: Archiv Osterode, Chronik 507, Thomas Leim,
Karl-Heinz Münch, Barbara Scharf, Ludwig Scheuerlein, Wolfgang Schneider, Freidrich
Schreiber, Gabriele Steinbrich and Rainer Michael Schöck, and Jürgen Wilhelm.

Page i: Trial run of repaired Tiger 333 near Sanok. The shortage of spare parts often
resulted in the cannibalisation of damaged panzers to get others
operational again.
Pages ii–iii: View from the radio operator's hatch of a Tiger during the fighting
at Brody in the spring of 1944 (*see page 81, below*). The Tigers ahead have left broad
tracks over the lightly snowed ground.

CONTENTS

FOREWORD

During the course of the Second World War, the German Wehrmacht formed a total of fifteen heavy tank battalions (*schwere Panzer-Abteilung*) equipped with Tiger or King Tiger heavy tanks – twelve for the *Heer* (Army) and three for the *Waffen-SS*. In the decades since the war, a number of excellent memoirs from former Tiger-tank crews have appeared, including Otto Carius's *Tigers in the Mud* and Richard von Rosen's *Panzer Ace*. In addition, several unit histories about the various Tiger-tank battalions have also been published; in particular, J. J. Fedorowicz produced volumes on the combat histories of the 503rd, 507th and 508th Heavy Tank Battalions back in 2000–3. Helmut Schneider, who edited the earlier volume for Fedorowicz, has now returned with the updated *Tiger Battalion 507* by Greenhill. Schneider's history is a mix of diary entries, veteran accounts and contextual overview, which follow the men of schwere Panzer-Abteilung 507 from the unit's formation in October 1943 to its eventual dissolution in April 1945.

Schneider's *Tiger Battalion 507* is based on contributions from about a dozen different battalion veterans, mostly compiled in the period 1982–90. Schneider himself was an *Unteroffizier* (non-commissioned officer) in the battalion in 1943–4, serving as a driver, gunner and briefly as a tank commander. Other veterans who contributed accounts served in a variety of roles, including as tank crewmen and in the workshop (*Werkstatt*) company.

The initial chapter lays out the organisation of the battalion in great detail, including its support elements. By the time that s. Pz. Abt. 507 began forming, the Third Reich was already hard pressed on all fronts and the veterans' accounts note the chaotic pace at which the battalion was formed in Germany and Holland, then shipped forthwith to the Eastern Front in March 1944. The battalion was literally deployed from its rail cars and sent directly into its first battle – the attempted relief of the encircled Tarnopol garrison. The Tarnopol action was fought under extremely adverse conditions, in freezing cold temperatures that made the inside of the Tigers feel 'just like a refrigerator'. Nevertheless, the battalion managed to spearhead an advance that pushed through Soviet lines and inflicted heavy losses on the enemy. However, the German veterans do not mention that the mission ended in failure – the relief effort never reached Tarnopol and the 4,000-man garrison was annihilated. Indeed, like many German veterans' accounts, the emphasis is placed more on damage inflicted on the enemy, rather than the fact that the Wehrmacht was being steadily pushed back toward the Reich.

The combat accounts and vignettes presented in *Tiger Battalion 507* are first-rate and quite candid. One veteran mentions backing his tank up too fast and accidentally running over some German infantry who did not get out of the way in time. Tank versus tank combat is described in fast-paced terms, with enemy shells whizzing by or slamming into the Tiger's thick armoured hide, while German gunners frantically train their sights on multiple opponents, knocking each out in turn. Although many of the crews were quite young, s. Pz. Abt. 507 had a solid core of veterans who held the battalion together and took a terrible toll on the enemy; in one three-day period in January 1945 the battalion was credited with knocking out 136 Soviet tanks. It is also interesting to see the personal side of war through the eyes of the men in s. Pz. Abt. 507, who linger thoughtfully on comrades killed in action or other small incidents, including some humorous ones. At one point, Schneider was disturbed that a sweater his mother gave him was torn to ribbons by enemy fire. Elsewhere, German tankers are overjoyed to find bacon hidden by peasants – such are the simple joys and frustrations of front-line life.

One of the more intriguing aspects of *Tiger Battalion 507* is the emphasis on the maintenance elements. The book has many photos and accounts of repair work in the field, which is not always present in armour unit histories. As a former tanker myself, I can attest that the kind of tank-recovery operations in frozen mud and snow that the veterans discuss are unforgettable experiences. Indeed, it is interesting to see from these accounts how frequently the Tigers threw track – either because of soft ground or mines – and the difficulty of track repair on the front line. The Tiger did not perform particularly well on soft ground due to its excessive weight, but the German Army High Command (OKH) apparently disregarded terrain factors when it sent units like s. Pz. Abt. 507 into marshy areas. Later, in February 1945, a similar disregard for the Tiger's limitations on crossing water obstacles led to twenty-two Tigers being blown up by their crews, because no provision had been made to get them across the Vistula River. Another aspect mentioned on several occasions is the lengthy time required to refill the Tiger's 540-litre fuel tank with 20-litre cans; Germany built a very advanced heavy tank but relied on rather primitive means to keep it supplied.

By the summer of 1944, s. Pz. Abt. 507 was hard pressed, as the Wehrmacht reeled backward into Poland as a result of the Soviet *Bagration* offensive. Increasingly, the battalion was not employed as a single formation, but rather operated as single companies in support of different infantry units. However, once the Eastern Front stabilised later in 1944, the situation changed and the tank crews became 'underground dwellers', living in bunkers near their Tiger tanks. Indeed, some crews even had time to help with the harvest and it is clear that the battalion was never short of food or booze. Attached to one infantry unit, the Tiger crews informed the local commander that they were supposed to receive a daily ration of schnapps – which they got! Compared to other branches of military service, tankers have a well-deserved reputation for seeking out creature comforts, at which the veterans of s. Pz. Abt. 507 were quite adept.

Most accounts about the Tiger tank focus on its magnificent 8.8 cm gun and there is plenty of evidence of its lethality presented in *Tiger Battalion 507*. Although the German tankers were concerned about the new Soviet JS-2 heavy tank, it appears that in most actions involving these vehicles, the Tigers had a distinct edge. The German veterans ascribe the superiority of the Tiger's gunnery to better training and the fact that the unitary 8.8 cm armour-piercing round could be loaded much quicker than the separate-loading (projectile and propellant were separate) ammunition used by the JS-2. Readers should be aware that old soldiers have a tendency to enlarge on their experiences and some of the veterans of s. Pz. Abt. 507 repeat some rather apocryphal stories, such as a claim that one of their Tigers destroyed a T-34 at a range of 8,000 metres. Such a claim was well beyond what tank sights in 1944 could discern, and even with modern technology the longest tank 'kill' on record is 'only' 4,700 metres, achieved by a British Challenger tank during the 1991 Gulf War. On the other hand, the Tiger was continually bedevilled by enemy mines and the Soviets – even when on the offensive – learned to plant mines to thwart German armoured counter-attacks. In one relief action near Brody, the battalion lost five of six Tigers involved to mine damage. While the Tiger was a capable fighting machine, by 1944 it was increasingly operating on its own with limited support from infantry, engineers and artillery, which reduced its overall impact on the battlefield.

By February 1945, s. Pz. Abt. 507 had very few Tigers left and most of the battalion was sent back to Paderborn to re-equip with the King Tiger tank. However, only one company had received its new King Tigers by the time that U.S. armoured units approached Paderborn in late March 1945. A scratch unit was hastily formed, under SS command, and the veterans of s. Pz. Abt. 507 fought their last major action against Task Force Welborn (3rd Armored

Division) on 30 March. The King Tigers inflicted a stinging tactical defeat on the U.S. column but it was irrelevant, since the training station at Paderborn was soon overrun and the battalion itself had essentially ceased to exist by early April 1945. It is noteworthy that the scratch unit formed at Paderborn, lacking maintenance support sub-units, could not operate for very long; many of its King Tigers were lost to minor technical defects.

Tiger Battalion 507 provides interesting insights into the daily life of German tank crews in 1944–5. In particular, the small-unit camaraderie and skilled leadership really come across as the critical factors which held s. Pz. Abt. 507 together, despite it operating under heavy enemy pressure and a deteriorating wartime situation. Although, as in most German post-war accounts, the authors try to avoid including any political viewpoints, it is clear that these veterans felt a great deal of pride in both their wartime service and their battalion's reputation. Schneider manages to sneak a passing reference to fighting 'for a supposed good cause' into his introduction, but otherwise there is little mention of the regime that s. Pz. Abt. 507 was fighting to preserve. While post-war accounts such as *Tiger Battalion 507* are important for assembling these first-person records before these veterans passed away, it is also important to remember that much of what is related in the book offers a somewhat 'sanitised' view of events, in order not to disturb modern sensibilities or impugn any members of the battalion. Oddly, there is no real mention of military misconduct or even desertions, although some of that must have been going on in the last few weeks of the war, particularly when it was evident that the war was lost and the unit virtually disintegrated. Truth, as often in historical narrative, can remain an elusive quantity.

Robert Forczyk

PREFACE

———

This is the story of Heavy Panzer (Tiger) Battalion 507, a military unit which existed for 500 days until its dissolution just before the Third Reich capitulated. What motivated a number of its former members to club together and commit their experiences to paper after so many years?

One of the reasons is that although Panzer Battalion 507 received mention in the third edition of *Tiger – die Geschichte einer legendären Waffe 1942–1945* by Egon Kleine and Volkmar Kühn (pages 294–9), its treatment in comparison with nearly all the other battalions was meagre because the two authors had so little material available. In a letter dated 4 February 1974, the first commanding officer of 507, Major Erich Schmidt (d. 1977) had provided Egon Kleine with some information about his Tiger battalion, but this had not been enlarged on by the time the third edition of that book was published.

Contacts pursued between the years 1977 and 1982 led to more and more former 507 men coming forward from the anonymity of post-war life. After a number of meetings held primarily by 2nd Panzer Division and Panzer Regiment 4 veterans, the first major reunion of former 507 panzer men was held at Rohrdorf/Inntal where it was decided to set up an editorial team to work at expanding the existing material on Panzer Battalion 507.

Leading this team were former Leutnant Dr Hans Maul and Captain (Reserve) Wolf Koltermann, the latter having made great efforts to set up a 'gathering of former members', especially from his 3rd Company. His circulars, and lists of names compiled from memory and sent by Kurt Kramer and Heinz Zinke much earlier from Russian captivity, led to a growing number of former comrades-in-arms becoming identified and located, and these then swelled attendances at the biannual reunions.

Meanwhile I, Helmut Schneider, had made a point of writing to all known former colleagues for the purpose of keeping us united and if possible enlarging our numbers; also to stimulate our powers of recall. Thus in later years the jigsaw was gradually put together with photographs, diary entries, letters, battlefield attestations and certificates accompanying the award of badges, medals and decorations, *Soldbuch* entries, leave passes, wartime newspaper cuttings, Wehrmacht bulletins and naturally accounts of personal experiences. Post-war literature was also used to prompt memories.

During the nine years which passed since our resolution in 1982 to write the '507' story, very many of our comrades-in-arms have left us for ever, amongst them our editor-in-chief Dr Hans Maul. The fact that all sources of recall had run dry spurred us to proceed on the basis of what we had, and in 1990 the 'Göttingen editorial team' confirmed that decision.

What individual authors had contributed in the form of diary extracts, personal experiences and aphorisms had to be assembled chronologically as soon as possible. Because the battalion had never been deployed as a single force, it was clear that reports from front-line companies, staff company platoons, the workshop company, the repairs staffs and the supply unit would all come from a totally different perspective. Even the five men sitting in the same panzer perceived or were affected by any event differently, and as for being certain of the geographical location, nobody ever kept a large-scale map of the area in which he was spending every day and night for weeks under the most unfavourable conditions!

This book sticks to retelling what our 'blood brotherhood' honestly experienced. It is meant to be a record for posterity, but above all a memorial for those comrades-in-arms who in faithful fulfilment of duty laid down their lives for a supposed good cause. Since the personal accounts are not confined to describing only what happened on the battlefield, but also other occurrences and impressions, not least the confusion of retreat, panic-stricken flight and captivity, it is also, so to speak, a collection of 'partial autobiographies' of a generation which sacrificed its best years to the war.

May the army of millions of dead of all nations bear witness to humanity for the hope that future generations may learn to discard war as the best way to resolve their differences.

Helmut Schneider

NOTE ON GEOGRAPHICAL NAMES

The original German-language text of this book naturally enough used the spellings familiar from wartime to the veterans of Heavy Panzer Battalion 507. Where an obvious English-language equivalent exists this has been preferred in this translation (*Vistula*, rather than the German *Weichsel* or the Polish *Wisła*, for example), but generally speaking the spellings used in the original accounts have been preserved. Selected German spellings and their modern equivalents are listed below.

Altdamm (Stettin)	Dąbie	Konitz	Chojnice
Augustov	Augustów	Köslin	Koszalin
Baranovicze	Baranavichy	Kowel	Kovel
Berent	Kościerzyna	Lemberg	Lviv
Bobruisk	Babruysk	Mackeim	Maków
Bütow	Bytów	Marienwerder	Kwidzyn
Cherson	Kherson	Mewe	Gniew
Chrzanov	Chrzanów	Mielau	Mława
Chrustov	Chrustowo	Mius	Miyc
Deutsch Eylau	Iława	Neidenburg	Nidzica
Dubze	Duże	Neufahrwasser	Nowy Port
Fastov	Fastiv	Ordzhonikidze	Vladikavkaz
Garnsee	Gardeja	Ortelsburg	Szczytno
Gollnow	Goleniów	Ostenburg	Pułtusk
Gotenhafen	Gdynia	Osterwitt	Ostrowitt
Graudenz	Grudziądz	Plöhnen	Płońsk
Kanev	Kaniv	Podhorce	Pidhirtsi
Kleck	Kletsk	Praschnitz	Przasnysz
Kolberg	Kołobrzeg	Preussisch Stargard	Starogard
Konarzev	Konarzewo		Gdański

Pripet	Pripyat	Sluzk	Slutsk
Rehden	Radzyń	Stettin	Szczecin
	Chełmiński	Stolp	Słupsk
Rippin	Rypin	Suchodole	Suchodół
Saporoshye	Zaporozhye	Tarnopol	Ternopil'
Scharfenwiese	Ostrołęka	Vinnica	Vinnytsia
Schröttersburg	Płock	Volkovysk	Vawkavysk
Schwetz	Świecie	Zambrov	Zambrów
Sichelberg	Sierpc	Zborov	Zborów
Schlawe	Sławno	Zichenau	Ciechanów

INTRODUCTION

I was born on 29 March 1922 at Hagen, North-Rhine Westphalia, a few miles south of Dortmund. My secondary school was at Rheydt, one of whose 'Old Boys' was Joseph Goebbels. At the age of nineteen I was granted my *Abitur* – the school-leaving certificate which qualified the holder for university and also an Army officer's career.

I volunteered for the panzer arm and was sworn in at Paderborn in May 1941. Four weeks' basic infantry training was followed by driving instruction on the Panzer I chassis. I qualified for panzer driving school by proving I could make a standing jump on to a tabletop while keeping both legs together. I passed the driving test and was also licensed to drive the ex-Czech tank Panzer 38(*t*).

A driving-school Panzer I chassis used for training, seen crossing a brook at Guntramsdorf.

A Panzer III with the long 5 cm L/60 gun seen at Rostov, June 1942.
In the advance to the Caucasus the author served mainly as driver or gunner
in this type. The gun was more powerful than the short-barrelled version
but did not guarantee success against the T-34.

Operation Barbarossa had begun on 22 June 1941 and I was one of the first
five men (all panzer-qualified drivers) to be sent to the Eastern Front as part
of a battalion being formed at Wuppertal by the Paderborn panzer barracks.
We five were allocated to 5th Company, Panzer-Ersatz-Abteilung 11 of 1st
Company, Panzer Regiment 4.

The objective was the Caucasus oilfields. By 11 October we had reached
Mariupol on the Sea of Azov. On 16 December 1941 I continued training in
the field with 2nd Battalion, Panzer Regiment 4. By 1 February 1942 when
I was upgraded to *Gefreiter* (trained private soldier) I had still seen no action.
Three months later, on 7 May, I was sent on the course for (wartime) officer-
candidates held at Grigoryenka.

I returned to my unit at Rostov on Don in July 1942. On 9 August we
entered Maikop in the foothills of the Caucasus. Besides driving I served
occasionally as a panzer gunner, mostly on Panzer IIIs, both those with
short- and long-barrelled guns. On 22 August we passed by Mount Elbrus,
the highest mountain in Europe.

Finally, on 6 September 1942, I had my first experience of a panzer attack. On 14 October 1942 as gunner of tank number 405 I was credited with the destruction of two enemy tanks and one anti-tank gun, plus some machine guns and anti-tank rifles. Next day, serving with 4th Company, Panzer Regiment 4, 13th Panzer Division, I received the Panzer Assault Badge for twelve attacks. Later that month we reached Ordzhonikidze, the most easterly and southerly point ever reached by the Wehrmacht advance. It was there that, on 12 November 1942, the campaign to destroy the Soviet oilfields was abandoned and we turned back. The reason was the disaster at Stalingrad and the possibility that the Russians intended to isolate the entire Caucasus region at Rostov. Thus we gave up the huge area we had conquered. On 15 November I commanded a tank for the first time, a Panzer III numbered 431.

By 12 December there was talk in the unit of a 'Deutschland-Kommando' – a group to be sent on home service – for which sixty men had been selected. I was not amongst them. On 24 December I was notified of the award of the Iron Cross Second Class but that the decoration was being withheld by Leutnant Gruss for some mysterious reason until the 'Deutschland-Kommando' had gone. For the remaining men there now began a period of

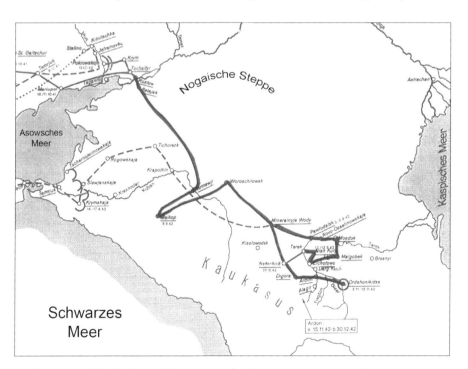

The route of 13th Panzer Division, with which the author served, towards the oilfields on the Caspian Sea, late 1941/1942. The campaign was called off at Ordzhonikidze on 12 November 1942.

In the summer of 1942, during the Wehrmacht advance into the Caucasus, the German Army crossed from Europe into Asia, as this propaganda photo shows.

refresher training prior to the great retreat from the Caucasus beginning on 1 January 1943. The 'Deutschland-Kommando' had already left for Germany where they would form the nucleus of Heavy Panzer Battalion 502.

On 3 February 1943 we learned that 4th Company, Panzer Regiment 4, was to be disbanded and its fifteen crews re-formed into an 'infantry intervention group': it was rumoured that we were to be flown out and given new panzers. This was true – apart from the new panzers. We went to the Crimea aboard He 111s towing heavy Gotha gliders and were accommodated in a kind of makeshift garrison at Stary Krym. It was a pleasant place far from the war. After a month's home leave I was sent on the NCOs' course starting 21 June. On 3 July I passed the driving test for heavy lorries.

During July 1943 we were moved up to the Kuban bridgehead in the expectation of some action but all remained quiet and we returned to barracks on 9 August. Meanwhile, recruits had arrived as reinforcements and I was made their Hut Senior. This appointment was combined with responsibility for supervising a party of civilians caring for the local cemetery.

On 18 August the latrine gossip now hinted at the operational section of the regiment having to leave Stary Krym for Germany: as if in confirmation on 9 September 1943 we were given three weeks' special home leave. There had been a heavy air raid on Rheydt at the end of August in which my family lost everything and so I gave my address as that of my grandparents at Bad Ems.

During the advance of Panzer Regiment 4 towards the Caucasian oilfields
in the summer of 1942, this photo of Mount Elbrus was taken
from the lowlands in passing.

Chapter 1

FORMATION AND INDUCTION, HEAVY PANZER BATTALION 507

The period of time covered in this chapter extends from October 1943 to March 1944. As a result of the disaster at Stalingrad and giving up the Caucasus the German front line, particularly the southern sector, had been greatly shortened. Nevertheless, following the offensive by the Ukrainian fronts in January 1944, it was anything but stable, not least because of the massive thinning out as a consequence of the expected invasion in France.

'The wheels must roll for Victory!' – an optimistic message on an early-war train.

Large areas of Soviet territory conquered by the Wehrmacht in the summer of 1941, shortly after the beginning of Operation Barbarossa, had long since had to be abandoned. The overall situation provided few signs giving rise to optimism. Despite that, we men of the panzer arm could look forward to the new panzer of which much had been predicted and for which selected men had been picked out since the beginning of 1943. We had convinced ourselves that, if handled correctly, its armour and firepower would provide a kind of life insurance!

The initial mustering of personnel for Heavy Panzer Battalion 507 took place in Vienna. Officers, NCOs and men forming the nucleus came from Panzer Regiment 4, its Reserve and Training Battalion, and from Reserve Battalion 500 at Paderborn, which had meanwhile become 'the home port of all Tiger battalions'. The distribution of the available personnel

Rail transport in the autumn of 1943 for members of 1st Battalion, Panzer Regiment 4, from Vienna to Angers in France to join personnel of Heavy Panzer Battalion 507. The photo shows Karl Krestan (1) and Heinz Zinke (2) at the wagon doors.

into companies and specific roles would take place later, once the instruction at Paderborn had begun.

When Gefreiter Helmut Schneider returned to Maria Enzersdorf at the end of his 'bombed-out leave' on 24 October 1943, the entire battalion had already moved on from Vienna. Reserve and Training Battalion 4 at Mödling, to which Schneider first reported, had no precise knowledge as to the whereabouts of his company and battalion but spoke vaguely of a 'deployment to Italy'. Sensing that this was a prelude to his being pocketed by the Mödling Battalion he made his excuses and left for the Frontsammelstelle (Front Assembly Post) from where he was directed to the Frontleitstelle (Front Control Post) in Paris.

By this point, Schneider had experience of a chaotic organisation. We take up his diary entries:

25 October 1943

I took a train from Vienna to Mulhouse in Alsace. Here I tarried awhile before I got the Paris express at the crack of dawn. The Paris Frontleitstelle told me to wait. I did some sightseeing.

28 October 1943

Frontleitstelle Paris told me to go by train to Rouen. I arrived there early next morning. Frontleitstelle Rouen, which took some finding, re-directed me to Le Mans.

29 October 1943

At Le Mans I was told to go to Angers. The next train was at 2300 hrs. I did some sightseeing first, then boarded the through-express for Nantes. I had a compartment to myself and fell asleep. I awoke just as we pulled away from Angers. Therefore I went on to Nantes and spent the remainder of the night in the Wehrmacht soldiers' hostel.

30 October 1943

My connection back to Angers left at 1100 hrs and arrived at 1300 hrs. An hour later I took the local stopping train to Baugé where the battalion was said to be located, but in fact only the staff company. Since nobody was going to my company today I went on a drinking bout and slept in the quarters of a boozing companion.

31 October 1943

A despatch rider of our company took me to Longué where the billets were dispersed across the village. I was shown to a gymnasium, home to fifty men. The life there was leisurely and the duties the best ever. When I reported to the commanding officer he told me I was scheduled for the Tiger commanders' course. The word 'course' always gave me a thrill, always something new to learn. It was a great honour for me as a *Gefreiter*, a private soldier, to be selected to command such a valuable fighting machine.

3 November 1943

The selected course participants were driven to Baugé where a train had been laid on to take us the same day to Paris and then down the Moselle stretch. On the fourth day we reached our destination at Paderborn. The town was the mustering garrison for the Tiger battalions while Panzer Regiment 11, the training and recruitment battalion, had been relocated to Bielefeld.

Late autumn 1943 at Le Mans, France: Heavy Panzer Battalion 507 was formed
near here from elements of 1st Battalion, Panzer Regiment 4, and other units.
It is not known if the château was used for accommodation purposes
or was merely visited as a local attraction.

7 November 1943

The course began with separation into three groups: panzer commanders,
gunners/loaders and radio operators. A special training course was planned
for drivers, workshop personnel and repair staffs. The commanders' group
consisted of officers and sergeants, three corporals and myself, a private.
Initially this caused me the problem of where to eat. I was not entitled to dine
in the officers' or NCOs' mess, and lower ranks ate at a different time. Finally
Unteroffizier Ziegeler managed to have me included as an honorary NCO in
his mess by virtue of my having been his classmate on the NCOs' course at
Stary Krym. Otherwise the course was very interesting and enjoyable.

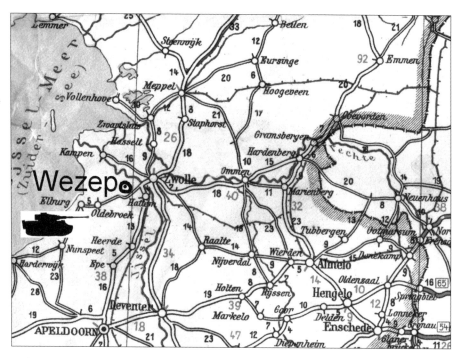

Map showing the location of the Troop Training Depot at Wezep near Zwolle
in Holland where Heavy Panzer Battalion 507 was brought up to strength
with Tigers and other vehicles.

15 November 1943

My parents came to visit and reserved good rooms in the town for a stay
of eight days. My duty hours, consisting of much instruction together with
practical training on the panzers, lasted from six in the morning until six at
night with one hour for lunch. I spent the evenings with my parents.

25 November 1943

The Tiger course ended. Everybody got leave, but only three days for me
because I had to attend the rangefinder course at Weimar. I spent my leave
quietly with my family at Rheydt.

29 November 1943

I took the 0800 hrs fast train to Weimar and met the other participants at
the artillery barracks; they included four Tiger commanders of the 507th:
Oberfähnrich (cadet senior grade) Dr Hans Maul, Oberfeldwebels (sergeant-
majors) Heinrich Diez and Fritz Breitfeld and Unterfeldwebel (sergeant)
Kolbe, this last man being previously unknown to me. The majority of those
on the course were artillerymen.

30 November 1943–3 January 1944

The rangefinder course consisted of theory and range measuring in the field. Because of frequent fog the practical side was often suspended, leaving us at liberty to go into town. The only attraction there was the parish fair with merry-go-round. On the bus ride back the nearest station was Buchenwald: all we knew of it was that the SS had a barracks there. This particular course was the most relaxed one I had been on and had the advantage of ending on 17 December.

We were given special leave extending into the New Year while those given leave from Paderborn had to report back shortly before Christmas. To my surprise while at home my promotion to *Unteroffizier* (corporal) came through and my mother sewed the lace on my shoulder straps as she had done the year before for my brother, recently fallen at the front. Another year of war had ended: the Eastern Front had moved much closer.

A factory-new Tiger I just arrived at Wezep. The turret is painted dark yellow, the outer and inner barrel jackets and the inner lining dark grey. Spare track sections have not yet been added to the front of the panzer.

4 January 1944

After my leave I had to return to Weimar to collect my stereoscopic rangefinder. It weighed 17 kg and was best carried slung across the shoulders. I took the train via Frankfurt/Main to Paris where the Frontleitstelle informed us that our unit had been transferred to Holland.

5 to 6 January 1944

On the 5th we took the train to Brussels and on the 6th went from there to Zwolle. The battalion was to be found at Oldebrouck Camp. The barracks at Wezep was like a village settlement with church, town hall and other official buildings naturally converted to military purposes.

When Schneider arrived at Wezep, sixteen of the battalion's Tigers were already present. According to the Bundesarchiv records, the following vehicles had been allocated and delivered to Heavy Panzer Battalion 507:

23 Dec. 1943:	6 Tigers	on train number 62953 83
24 Dec. 1943:	3 Tigers	on train number 62953 84
26 Dec. 1943:	7 Tigers	on train number 62953 85
20 Jan. 1944:	3 Tigers	on train number 64414 46
24 Feb. 1944:	12 Tigers	on train number 145 2003/4
25 Feb. 1944:	14 Tigers	on train number 145 2005/6

With these six trainloads bringing forty-five Tigers the battalion was at its full authorised establishment, and presumably at the same time the issue of half-tracked and wheeled vehicles had also been completed. From memory the posts were filled as follows:

Staff

Commanding Officer:	Major Erich Schmidt
Adjutant:	Oberleutnant Wolf Koltermann
Orderly Officer:	Leutnant Dr Hans Maul
Reconnaissance Platoon:	Leutnant Moser
Commander, Staff Company:	Oberleutnant Peter Heesch
Commander, 1st Company:	Hauptmann Siegfried Holzheid
Commander, 2nd Company:	Hauptmann Fritz Schöck
Commander, 3rd Company:	Oberleutnant Fritz Neumeyer

Officers of Heavy Panzer Battalion 507 at Wezep in December 1943.
From left to right: Oberleutnant Fritz Neumeyer (commander 3rd Company);
Hauptmann Siegfried Holzheid (commander 1st Company); Major Erich
Schmidt (commanding officer, Heavy Panzer Battalion 507); Oberleutnant Wolf
Koltermann, Adjutant, later commander 3rd Company; Hauptmann Fritz Schöck
(commander 2nd Company, later commanding officer, Heavy Panzer Battalion
507); and Oberleutnant Peter Heesch, Staff Platoon.

Commander, Workshop Company: Oberleutnant (Ing.) Helmut Küssner
Technical Controller: Oberleutnant (Ing.) Johann Steinborn

Platoon Leaders

1st Company

1st Platoon: Oberleutnant Rudi Beilfuss
2nd Platoon: Leutnant (?) Berthold
3rd Platoon: Oberfeldwebel (?) Rateyczak

2nd Company

1st Platoon: Oberleutnant Max Wirsching
2nd Platoon: Leutnant (?) Lischka
3rd Platoon: Feldwebel Rolf Gebhardt

3rd Company

1st Platoon:	Leutnant Bernhard Pfeuffer
2nd Platoon:	Leutnant Gerd Eychmüller
3rd Platoon:	Oberfeldwebel Heinrich Diez

Workshop Company

1st Workshop Platoon:	Oberwerkmeister Rutkowski
2nd Workshop Platoon:	Werkmeister Grüger

The Workshop was made up of armoury, salvage and security platoons and the spare parts stores. Changes to the plan during the war were caused mainly by the transfer of commanding officer Major Erich Schmidt to take command of the Panzer Regiment, Führer-Grenadier Brigade, and also the death of Hauptmann Fritz Neumeyer. Occasionally, on account of a shortage of panzers, not all platoon leader positions were filled. The essential posts were later occupied as follows:

Commanding Officer:	Major Fritz Schöck
Adjutant:	Oberleutnant Georg Reinhardt
ADC:	Lt Dieter Jähn
Commander, Staff Company:	Oberleutnant Peter Heesch
Commander, 1st Company:	Hauptmann Rudi Beilfuss
Commander, 2nd Company:	Hauptmann Max Wirsching
Commander, 3rd Company:	Hauptmann Wolf Koltermann
Supply Company:	Hauptmann Johann Baptist Müller
Workshop:	Oberleutnant (Ing.) Helmut Küssner

Other officers at the end of the war were: Oberleutnant Heinz Jähn, Leutnant Dr Hans Maul, Leutnant Gustl Stadler, Leutnant Heinrich Diez and Leutnant Helmut Schneider. Unteroffizier Schneider was detached to the Military Academy in June 1944, Oberfeldwebel Diez in the late summer. Once commissioned, neither returned to Panzer Battalion 507 and nor did Oberfeldwebel Rolf Gebhardt, holder of the German Cross in Gold and the Knight's Cross, who was sent to the Officer Cadet School at Gross-Glienicke as a *Fahnenjunker* (officer cadet senior grade).

After the appointments had been made and the vehicles became available, each man had to get to know the vehicle or the equipment which he would

Major Fritz Schöck, last commanding officer of Heavy Panzer Battalion 507.
He was awarded the German Cross in Gold on 8 January 1943 and the
Knight's Cross on 5 September 1944.

now operate. An intensive period of familiarisation now began, which for the
Tiger crews consisted of applying in practice the theory absorbed from the
Tiger manual and gaining the necessary experience. This was very interesting
because the Tiger technology was innovative and had many new advantages:

Front page of the propaganda journal *Signal*, published in various languages in the
occupied territories in the West. This French edition has the caption: 'This latest
model German tank has already made its appearance on all fronts.'

what would most panzer drivers have given for such a steering system as this, the gunners for such a rotating turret or such optics, not to mention the gun! The training of technical personnel and drivers is recalled from their individual perspectives by Richard Durst, Helmut Küssner and Helmut Schneider:

Richard Durst

We were given leave on arriving in Vienna, and when I reported back I was sent to Kassel where the Tigers were completed and assembled at the firm of Henschel. I was supposed to attend a course on the structure of the Tiger I but since all courses were full I was put to work as a turner.

The big air raid on Kassel on 23 October 1943 left the town in flames from end to end and I spent several days running rations from the barracks to the clearance squads at the Henschel works. A Hauptmann Klatt always accompanied me there. Later at Henschel I had to take over 'the late shift' – Belgians working in a suburb of Kassel. After that I went on the Tiger course at Paderborn, and when we received our equipment in the Netherlands, I was naturally a member of the repair staff again, attached to 3rd Company, Panzer Battalion 507.

Helmut Küssner

After we finished the administration and mustering of personnel near Angers in December 1943, a number of complete panzer crews were sent to Magdeburg with myself as technical leader. There we had to take charge of the first Tiger tanks from an army supplies office and bring them to the new centre at Zwolle. From the technical point of view I had to practise changing tracks from the wider field tracks to the transport tracks prior to loading aboard rail lowloaders using a 'transportable loading head ramp'.[1]

The Workshop Company had an authorised establishment of 240 men but this was never attained during the formative period. It consisted of two

---

1. Field tracks reduced the pressure of the panzer on the ground by spreading the weight over a greater surface area. However, the Tiger was 3.55 m wide with field tracks: this exceeded the width limit for rail transport except on single-track branch lines or on two-way working where oncoming trains had been halted. . The transport tracks were part of the Ssyms-wagon inventory. For rail journeys they were fitted in place of the field tracks and, after the eight outer running wheels had been removed, the panzer would be hauled up the boarding ramp onto the wagon. To prevent two neighbouring wagons from tilting up during this operation, which would cause the axle pins of the wheel pairings to slip out of their bearings, rail clamps hanging in the wagon couplings were tied to the rails and lashed down during the loading.

Leutnant Hans Steinborn (*left*) and Oberleutnant Helmut Küssner of the
Workshop Company. Without them and their industrious teams, the Tigers would
soon have been helpless.

workshop platoons, the armourer's platoon, the radio equipment platoon, the recovery platoon and a security platoon.

No. 1 Workshop Platoon, under the technical direction of Oberwerkmeister Rutkowski, carried out major repairs and therefore operated mainly in the rear areas. No. 2 Workshop Platoon under Werkmeister Grüger generally worked closer to the front line. His spare parts staff maintained amongst other things a store of replacement engines and gearboxes. Thanks to good 'organisation' this reserve was much greater than our entitlement so that no Tiger ever needed to leave the battalion on account of engine or transmission damage. Feldwebel Schneider used to wait with some men in a lorry at the army-level spare parts compound in order to 'buy in' spare parts and materials for our battalion in excess of its needs. This ensured that the repair section never had a bottleneck due to shortages!

Specialists with the armourer's and radio equipment platoons would look over every Tiger brought into the workshops. Every workshop platoon had two workshop vehicles, plus two more for materials, two for electro-welding, a portal crane and a crane on a towing-tractor chassis. There was also a workshop marquee in which six Tigers could be repaired simultaneously.

The recovery platoon had eight 18-tonne tractors, two for each recovery squad, since it required two such tractors to tow a 57-tonne Tiger I on extended countershafts on a flat road surface.

The workshop platoon also kept sufficient provisions to feed the idle crews of those Tigers under repair.

Helmut Schneider

In those days we got to know a special unit which operated remote-controlled 'P4' panzers. For some time it was expected that in action every Tiger commander would 'pull the strings' of two midget panzers loaded with explosives. The idea was eventually rejected as crazy. The P4 was fitted with an automatic stop device which activated if the panzer did not receive a signalled instruction within twenty seconds of the preceding one. During a field exercise the device aboard one P4 had not been plugged in and in undulating country the small, low-profile panzer disappeared from sight to continue beyond signal range. It arrived at a railway line and, followed at a cautious distance by a train, proceeded to the next station where the engine stalled at the points.

In mid-February 1944 I was transferred as an instructor to a Waffen-SS panzer unit located at Kampen on the Zuyder Zee. I was not wanted there and they sent me on five days' immediate leave. I spent three full days of this leave on trains: Kampen–Zwolle–Arnhem–Emmerich–Oberhausen–Duisburg–Cologne–Regensburg–Landshut–Moosburg and had to change trains eight times. Now I knew how things stood in the 'spare parts homeland'! When I reported back to battalion and my commanding officer heard that I had been sent on leave in this way he almost fell off his stool. Then he took my *Soldbuch* and struck out this leave as 'not taken'!

Once all vehicles had arrived we had exercises en masse. At the beginning of March 1944 we held a major exercise with the *Hermann Göring* Division stationed nearby. Amongst its prominent guests were Guderian, Inspector of Panzer Troops; Christiansen, Military Plenipotentiary for the Netherlands; Seyss-Inquart, Reich Commissioner for the Netherlands; and Generaloberst Beck (committed suicide, night of 20 July 1944). Much praise from amongst all the cigar smoke!

Makeup of Panzer Battalion 507

'NCO' means *Unteroffizier* (corporal) and above: 'Official' is a non-Wehrmacht designation. A Kfz. 1 is a military staff car.

1st Battalion Staff: 9 officers, 4 NCOs and 12 men

2. Staff Company:

(I)   *1st Company Squad* (Group Leader) – 1 officer, 1 NCO, 2 men
(II)   *Armoured Reconnaissance Platoon* – 1 officer, 7 NCOs, 33 men.
(III)   *Signals Platoon* – 1 officer, 12 NCOs, 6 men
         3 command panzers (CO, Adjutant and ADC) and one motorcycle
(IV)   *Short-range Reconnaissance Platoon* – 1 officer, 4 NCOs, 21 men
         Platoon squad: 3 motorcycles, 1 × Kfz. 1
         3 squads with one motorcycle and 2 × Kfz. 1 each
(V)   *Pioneer Platoon* – 4 NCOs, 21 men
         1 motorcycle, one amphibious VW, 2 lorries, 2 armoured vehicles
(VI)   *Flak Platoon*
         3 motorcycles, 1 × Kfz. 15, 3 motorised quadruple flak, 3 ammunition trailers
(VII)   *Kfz. Repair Staff*
         2 Kfz. 1, 1 Kfz. 2/40 (welding gear), 1 × 3-tonne lorry, 2 lifting cranes (3- and 6-tonnes), 2 × 4.5-tonne lorries with machinery, 1 × 1-tonne tractor.
(VIII)   *Recovery Group*
         1 × Kfz. 15, 2 × 35-tonne tractors, 3 × 4.5-tonne lorries for ammunition, etc.

(IX)   Tross I (Rearward Support Staff)
   2 × Kfz. 1, 2 × 4.5-tonne tankers, 2 × 4.5-tonne lorries for ammunition, etc.
(X)   Medical Team
   1 motorcycle, 2 × Kfz. 31 ambulances, 1 medical officer's panzer

Strength: IX and X combined: 7 NCOs, 21 men

(XI)   Tross II
   1 × 3-tonne lorry
(XII)   Admin and Supply Staff – 2 officials, 10 NCOs, 73 men
   1 motorcycle, 3 × Kfz. 1, 1 × 3-tonne field kitchen, 10 × 4.5-tonne tankers,
   20 × M-Lkw lorries
(XIII)   Provisions Unit
   2 × 4.5-tonne lorries, 1 Kfz. 1.
(XIV)   Baggage Train
   1 × 3-tonne lorry

3. Three Heavy Panzer Companies each with:

Group Leader: 2 × Panzer VI Tiger I; 1 Kfz. 1, 3 motorcycles, 1 motorcycle
                and sidecar, one bicycle.
1st Platoon: 4 × Pz VI Tiger I (1 officer, 7 NCOs, 12 men)
2nd Platoon: 4 × Pz VI Tiger I (1 officer, 5 NCOs, 14 men)
3rd Platoon: 4 × Pz VI Tiger I (6 NCOs, 14 men)
Repair troop: 4 × Kfz. 1, 2 lorries (3.5-tonne and 4.5 tonne), 2 × 1-tonne
                tractors
Gefechtstross I (Close Support Staff)
                1 bicycle, 1 motorcycle and sidecar, 2 Kfz. 1, 6 × 3-tonne
                lorries
Gefechtstross II: 1 bicycle, 1 × 3-tonne lorry
Baggage Train: 1 × 3-tonne lorry

4. Workshop Company

Group Leader: 3 × Kfz. 1; 2 officers, 1 official, 1 NCO, 9 men
1 and 2 Groups: 3 × 4.5-tonne lorries, 8 × 4.5-tonne lorries for spare
   parts, 2 × 4.5-tonne lorries workshop equipment, 2 × 4.5-tonne lorries
   machinery, 1 × 3-tonne swing crane, 1 × 10-tonne swing crane; 1 official,
   9 NCOs, 47 men
Recovery Platoon: 3 × Kfz. 1, 2 swing cranes (3-tonne and 10-tonne),
   2 towing vehicles with low-loader; 1 officer, 15 NCOs, 25 men
Armoury: 2 × Kfz. 1, 2 × 4.5-tonne lorries for equipment; 2 officials, 2 NCOs,
   12 men

Workshop for Signals Equipment: 1 × 4.5-tonne lorry for signals equipment, 1 × 3-tonne lorry for radio equipment, 1 × 4.5-tonne lorry for battery chargers; 2 NCOs, 5 men

Tross Workshop Company: 2 × Kfz. 1, 2 field kitchens, 1 air-raid protection VW amphibious vehicle, 1 × 4.5-tonne lorry for men and equipment, 2 × 4.5-tonne lorries for fuel

Trials were made at Wezep to see if a Tiger commander could operate two radio-controlled P4 tanks to clear obstacles, bunkers and so on. The project was found to be impracticable and was abandoned.

Heavy Panzer Battalion 507 was transferred from Holland to the Eastern Front in March 1944. This photo was taken on the way to Lemberg. The Tigers are already fitted with broad tracks.

The successful Panzer Battalion 507 was founded on men like these,
seen relaxing outside a French château.

Many soldiers absorbed into Panzer Battalion 507 were veteran panzer men with experience of the Russian Front.

Major Erich Schmidt was the first commanding officer of Heavy Panzer Battalion 507. He was awarded the German Cross in Gold on 30 May 1942 and the Knight's Cross on 9 June 1944.

Officers of the battalion. *From left:* Heesch, Holzheid, Schmidt, Koltermann, Schöck and Neumeyer at Wezep, January 1944, with Tiger 231 behind them.

Generalmajor Dr Fritz Bäke commanded the Panzer Division
Feldherrnhalle 2 after serving as a battalion commander
in Panzer Regiment 11.

Hauptmann Siegfried Holzheid as commander 1st Company in Tiger 101
at Wezep. As a result of experience gained in Russia, all Tigers were fitted with
additional spare track sections at the front and on the turret
for increased protection.

Generaloberst Guderian, Inspector of Panzer Troops, visited Heavy Panzer Battalion 507 at Wezep in March 1944 shortly before it moved out to the Eastern Front. *From right:* Neumeyer, Guderian, Schmidt (battalion commander), Holzheid. To the left are two of Guderian's ADCs.

A VW-Kübelwagen of the battalion on the cobbled road between Wezep and Zwolle.

Leutnant Moser (*left*) of the Reconnaissance Platoon and Leutnant Dr Maul as orderly officer composed and wrote the lyrics for the 507 *Tigerlied*.

The Panzer V Panther was based to some extent on the Soviet T-34 tank. After overcoming some defects in quality at the beginning of series production, in the period 1943–5 the Panther developed into one of the most important panzers.

A Soviet SU-76 tank destroyer seen near the wreck of a Panzer IV.

A heavy Josef Stalin 2 (JS-2) tank armed with a 12.2 cm gun carrying infantry
on the hull during an advance. 507 Panzer Battalion had to grapple with
heavy tanks of this kind in January 1945.

The wreck of a Soviet SU-152 self-propelled gun.
This heavy assault gun was a dangerous opponent for a Tiger.

A German Nebelwerfer rocket battery in action. Because the firing position of these rockets could be seen from afar, the launching vehicles had to relocate immediately to avoid being targeted by enemy artillery or aircraft.

The Wespe (Sd.Kfz. 124) was a 10.5 cm field howitzer in an open-topped mounting on a Panzer Mk II chassis. Here a battery of the type is seen in firing position.

Tiger 111 of platoon leader Rudi Beilfuss with rolled carpeting of poles at the sides for letting down in swampy areas.

Aerial view of the new Tiger. The type was developed from mid-1942
as a heavy panzer for priority situations at the front. The first batches
arrived in the autumn of 1942.

Above right: The recovery platoon operated one-tonne Demag light half-tracks
to access immobilised Tigers in open country.
Right: An *Unteroffizier* of the repairs staff ('J' on pennant) of an unknown unit.

The masses of Soviet tanks deployed in the field could not be held in check by panzers and anti-tank guns alone. This Ju 87 Stuka dive-bomber is equipped with two 3.7 cm cannon below the wings for anti-tank work.

The Soviets used fighter-bombers to engage ground targets. The Il-2 Sturmovik seen here was much feared by German ground troops.

Chapter 2

FIRST OPERATIONS:
TARNOPOL–BRODY–KOWEL

In July 1943, at the time when the Army High Command was already planning the formation of Panzer Battalion 507, the last great German offensive in the east was raging north and south of Kursk. After the Army and Luftwaffe had been re-equipped with all available means, it was hoped to halt the endless round of defensive fighting and retreats and turn the tide in the east in Germany's favour. Ultimately it did no more than fatally weaken the fighting strength of the Wehrmacht. No sooner had Model's Ninth Army and Hoth's Fourth Army finally broken through the deeply echeloned Russian positions to a point where success seemed at least possible, the Russians appeared on the attack unexpectedly elsewhere.

On 12 July 1943 the Red Army broke through the German front north of Orel, and three days later also east of Orel, thus sealing the fate of the German attack north of the Kursk salient. This situation was repeated south of the salient on 17 July when the Russians broke through at Bervenkov on the central Donets, and crossed the Mius River. The very heavy losses suffered by the Wehrmacht during the Battle of Kursk had absorbed all the reserves and created the major problem of how the ominous gaps in the front were to be plugged.

Once the smoke had cleared it was obvious that the shrinking German divisions were having to face many more Russian divisions with enormously increased firepower. Looking at the artillery and panzers the German staffs now calculated that the ratio of forces favoured the Russians by six to one. The entire Eastern Front extending from Leningrad to Taganrog was held by units which had been thinned out to a dangerous level and were too weak almost everywhere to resist the enemy's massive pressure, and also had no reserves!

On 9 September 1943, after Model's Ninth Army had yielded Orel, the Red Army advanced at Byelgorod south of Kursk with a huge force of five armies and tore open the front over a distance of 45 km. Their next objective

The German Elefant Jagdpanzer (Sd.Kfz. 184) with the long 8.8 cm gun was used by a few heavy tank-destroyer battalions in 1943–4 but failed to live up to expectations.

was clear: the Dnieper and Kiev. The river south of Kiev is over 2 km wide, up to 12 m deep and has a steep slope on its western banks. The two most senior German commanders, Manstein (Army Group South) and Kluge (Army Group Centre) had recognised much earlier that here was the ideal interception point to tackle an enemy coming from the east. Führer-HQ (FHQ) rejected the idea and for a long period Hitler had forbidden the building of a 'Dnieper Position', reportedly basing his objection on the premise that 'All a developed fortified line will do is create the idea in the minds of my generals and troops that it is somewhere safe they can fall back to.'

Finally, in mid-August 1943, permission was given for an 'Eastwall on the Dnieper'. No workforce was made available to build it and so no progress was made. On 14 September in a signal to FHQ Manstein stated that it was possibly the intention of the Soviets to embark on a breakthrough to Kiev and Kremenchug, and in order to prevent Fourth Panzer Army being broken up into numerous small pockets and slaughtered he had ordered it to pull back on 15 September to the Dnieper. He also wanted to have Eighth Army and First Panzer Army brought back soon. FHQ replied: 'You may not give that order. The Führer expects you tomorrow for a conference.'

This fourth discussion between Hitler and Manstein within a month was brief and heated but Manstein got his way and received permission to pull the front back behind the Dnieper. To what extent that might be physically possible was another matter. Five bridges and the dam at Saporoshye, all potential bottlenecks, were the only possible routes Manstein had at his disposal to bring a million men and their equipment across the river and spread them out along 700 km of the Dnieper's western banks to form the new front.

The danger inherent in this retreat was demonstrated by the bitterly fought 'Race to the Dnieper' during which the Red Army seized the opportunity to thrust itself into the inevitable gaps which appeared as the German units struggled to the six crossing points. One might even speak of 'The Miracle of the Dnieper' when one reflects that the Russians failed to capture even one of the crossing points before Manstein got his army group across the river, for the most part safe and sound. However, the possibility of holding this strategic and economically important front in the long term was not guaranteed because the 'Eastwall' on the Dnieper with its fortifications on the west bank had not been built.

In the last week of September, the Red Army succeeded in crossing a 700 km stretch of the Dnieper at twenty-three places, establishing a small bridgehead at each. At one position 100 km north of Kiev where the Pripet flows into the Dnieper, a whole army got across. This had not been allowed

Lvóv in Poland (Lemberg in German, now Lviv in Ukraine) was occupied by the Germans in September 1939, ceded to the Soviets by the terms of the Hitler–Stalin Pact, retaken by the Germans in 1941, and regained by the Soviets in July 1944.

for by the German generals because the delta was amongst impassable swamp. What was not known was that partisans had been working for months putting down secret log roads.

It required a great effort to deny the Russians any further encroachment. For a short while it even seemed that their advance to the Dnieper had been stopped but the lull did not last long: they stepped up their pressure on the 'Wotan Line', the defensive position between Saporoshye and Melitopol. On 15 October 1943 Saporoshye fell. Until then it had been held by XL Panzer Corps, maintaining a major bridgehead on the eastern bank of the Dnieper as flank protection for Sixth Army fighting to the south. The los ??????ed the collapse of the northern corner post of the Wotan Line and depriv? ?ixth Army of its cover on the flank. The loss of Melitopol to a numerically g ?atly superior force followed on 23 October. This tore open the German fron? 'ong a stretch of 45 km, allowing the enemy to head for the Dnieper delta v ?th a powerful spearhead and cut Sixth Army to pieces. Mixed groups fought ?ack

Sketch by a 507 Battalion artist at Lemberg on 1 May 1944.

Smudges of smoke on the horizon mark hits on enemy targets.

to behind the lower course of the Dnieper, a route over 200 km long from Melitopol to Cherson.

The evacuation of the Crimea, where the intact Seventeenth Army was almost cut off and condemned to operational inactivity, would still have been possible at this time but Hitler refused to release it 'for political reasons'. In the spring of 1944 all but 100 men of this army were lost as the result of Hitler's illusion that a large bridgehead could be held south-east of Nikopol on the far side of the Dnieper as the base for a later attack towards the Crimea.

The catastrophic year of 1943 was not over yet, however, for in the course of September and October the Russians succeeded in so greatly expanding one of their twenty-three small Dnieper bridgeheads just north of Kiev (near the village of Lyutesh) that they formed three armies and one armoured corps (with more than 2,500 guns and rocket launchers) to strike at the 'granary of the Ukraine'. On 3 November, after a powerful artillery barrage had softened up the three German divisions opposite, the Russians broke through stiffening resistance to a depth of 7–10 km. It remains a mystery why this deadly threat to Kiev was not foreseen, or if it had been why suitable counter-measures were not in place, unless it was simply the case that 'the shirt was too short'.

On 6 November 1943 the Soviets recaptured Kiev, but far worse for the Germans happened the next day when 3rd Guards Tank Army under General Rybalkov took the gigantic marshalling yards at Fastov 50 km south-west of

Kiev in a surprise attack and seized masses of rolling stock including forty-five locomotives. This was a logistical catastrophe for Army Group South; and Rybalov was now a major problem to the rear of Army Group von Manstein. Thus another supporting column of the Dnieper position had been pulled down.

In the offensive on 4 November, Rybalov had used an especially interesting tactic for the first time against the German panzer men which Erich Winhold described as follows:

'The battlefield was lit up, our ears rang with the crazy shrieking. Rybalov had swarms of T-34s roll towards us with blinding searchlights and howling sirens, and as they approached the German lines the T-34s kept firing. Crouching low on the tank hulls, not visible because of the searchlights, were their infantry – it was a hellish spectacle with a psychological effect. And it worked, psychologically and otherwise, for the firepower of those T-34s was enormous, and the thin German lines crumbled.'

Ploughed field lightly covered with snow, Brody battlefield, spring 1944.

By January 1944, Army Group South still held two small sections of the Dnieper bank, at Nikopol and Kanev (with its unique two-tier road/railway bridge), but neither mud nor frost had lessened the pressure of the Russian attack. There ensued a series of encircling actions in which the Russian attempts alternated with German break-outs and counter-attacks, both sides claiming success, from time to time. In mid-January the Russians began a major encirclement offensive aimed at surrounding Eighth Army. When the neck of the bag was closed at Svenigorodka at the end of the month, it trapped half of Eighth Army within it. Relieving attacks were unsuccessful. Over the next fourteen days the pocket, originally of 2,000 km², was compressed to 10 km² and was finally liquidated by the Russians on 17 February. Only half of those in the encirclement managed to escape to the west, leaving weapons and equipment behind.

The loss of six and a half divisions was an enormous disaster for Army Group South and prepared the way for a final catastrophe in the southern sector of the Eastern Front, for scarcely had a weak but cohesive front been set up running from the delta of the Dnieper to the Pripet marshes than the Russian armies renewed their offensive at the beginning of March 1944. One attack spearhead ran from the Uman area to the south-west led by Marshal Koniev, the other, from Rovno-Shepetovka heading south, was commanded by Marshal Zhukov. Farther south the armies of Marshal Malinovski proceeded unopposed to the southern Bug. A consequence of this major Soviet offensive was that in the northern sector of Army Group South contact between First Panzer Army and Fourth Panzer Army was lost and the right wing of the latter was forced westwards while strong enemy forces now wheeled south. Uman fell, and on 6 March when the enemy offensive against Army Group A (Feldmarschall von Kleist) began, the entire South-Eastern Front was set in motion over a width of 1,100 km.

From 23 March, therefore just three weeks later, the onset of the catastrophic development became clear. In the far south the German Sixth and Eighth Armies were practically destroyed, or at least routed: in the northern section Fourth Panzer Army's front was ruptured and forced well back to the west. First Panzer Army now sat in a gigantic pocket between the southern Bug and Dniester. If this force of twenty-two divisions – amongst them the

Propaganda Company photograph taken at the readiness position prior to the attack on Tarnopol. To the left, Staff Tiger A, at the centre Tiger 201, and to the right another Tiger and a Wespe self-propelled gun. From the hillside, Waffen-SS grenadiers watch the impressive assembling of the battle group.

best panzer divisions with around 200,000 men – were to be lost, little would stand in Stalin's way in his advance to the west.

General Hube, the one-armed commanding general of First Panzer Army, naturally recognised the danger and wanted to break out of the trap as soon as possible by heading south and crossing the Dniester. Here a gap had been identified with little Russian protection. Feldmarschall von Manstein, chief of the Army Group, refused his permission for fear that a break-out in that direction would only result in a fresh encirclement enabling the Russians to drive First Panzer Army against the Carpathian mountains. Manstein's concept was to have Hube break out to the west even though this meant his having to cross two rivers and go through two Russian armies. As he assessed the situation, only by re-uniting First Panzer Army and Fourth Panzer Army was there a prospect of stabilising the southern front while holding the line of the Carpathians. As he conceded, this would require a couple of fresh divisions for Fourth Panzer Army so that Hube would have a goal to work towards. On 23 March Manstein asked Hitler for these new divisions. Meanwhile Dubno and Vinniza had both been lost and Hitler also forbade any break-out of First Panzer Army to the south.

A destroyed 7.62 cm Soviet anti-tank gun, nicknamed the 'Ratch-boom'.
Panzer crews rated this gun as more dangerous than a T-34 tank
because it was harder to spot.

Crew of Tiger 223 after a trial run. The commander (*upper left*) wears the German Cross in Gold but his name is unknown. His gunner, an NCO (*extreme right*), is decorated with the Iron Cross First Class.

Chapter 3

ARRIVAL ON THE
EASTERN FRONT

WOLF KOLTERMANN: Panzer Battalion 507 had been loaded on nine railway trains – to where? Some thought initially to Italy, then there was talk of Hungary where it was important to bring a fickle ally to heel by means of Operation Margarete. When we finally de-trained at Krasne (east of Lemberg) on 21 March 1944, we saw that the Eastern Front had us once more in its clutches!'

The situation in this sector was as follows. A gap 40 km wide lay between Tarnopol and Brody. Tarnopol was surrounded, Brody under heavy enemy pressure. Panzer Battalion 507 was now subordinated to Panzer Verband *Friebe* for use as a 'fire brigade'. We had at our side 9th SS Panzer Division *Hohenstaufen*. At the time we were not aware that the situation was grave, indeed, fairly hopeless. Our 'communications' consisted of the intercom and Fu 5, the range of which was less than the visible horizon and also restricted to 'events close at hand', carefully choosing one's words so as not to provide the enemy with information and propaganda. Therefore we give contemporary notes free rein here.

First come the diary entries of Anton Seefried and Siegfried Obermayr (both of the Reconnaissance Platoon), and Helmut Schneider (3rd Company). These are followed in chronological order by the battle reports of Nietsch and Helmut Gutmann (2nd Company), and Leutnant Gerd Eychmüller and Franz Raab (3rd Company) as verified from *Soldbuch* entries signed by company commanders Fritz Schöck (2nd Company) and Fritz Neumeyer (3rd Company).

Calendar and Diary Entries

21 March 1944

SCHNEIDER: The beginning of spring, for me my third in Russia. Our transporter train, which left Zwolle on 16 March, reached Krasne today, a small town on the Lemberg–Tarnopol railway line where we were unloaded smartly. As we heard later, the leading Tigers headed for their first attack straight from the ramp.

SEEFRIED: We arrived at Krasne where unloading began at 1700 hrs. Then we drove down the *Rollbahn* to Dubze where the reconnaissance platoon spent its first night in enemy country. It snowed.

22 March 1944

SEEFRIED: We were awoken at 0400 hrs. It was fairly cold as we set out for Zloczov and Zborov for Jezierna. We got there at 1700 hrs and secured on the edge of town. The weather does not like us. An icy storm blew across the plain all night.

OBERMAYR: Moved up towards Brody and Olesko during the night. Horrible sight, everything on fire.

23 March 1944

OPERATIONAL ORDERS: '3rd Company advance to Cebrov and Kurovce.'

SEEFRIED: At 0400 the battalion headed towards the enemy for the first time. The objective was to clear enemy forces from the railway line to Tarnopol, and from the village of Jezierna. At the beginning of the attack there was some resistance which we crushed at once. As soon as they spotted us, the Russians fled from the railway line towards a hill where most fell under our fire. Then

The bold thrust led by Maximilian 'Max' Wirsching at Brody in January 1944 brought relief and enabled many wounded men to be brought out.

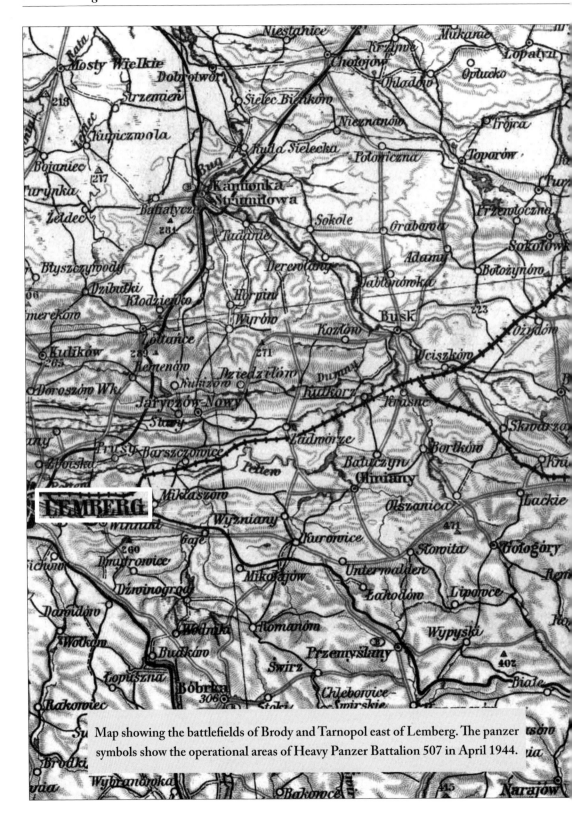

Map showing the battlefields of Brody and Tarnopol east of Lemberg. The panzer symbols show the operational areas of Heavy Panzer Battalion 507 in April 1944.

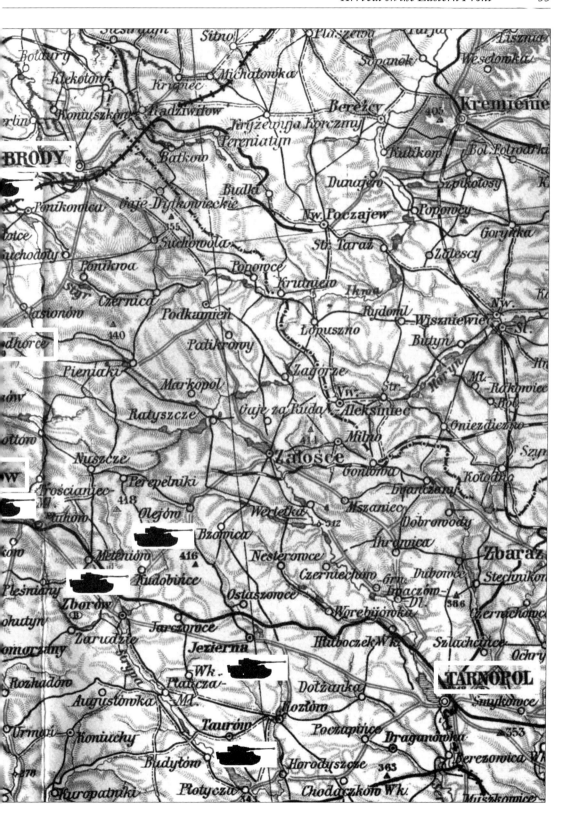

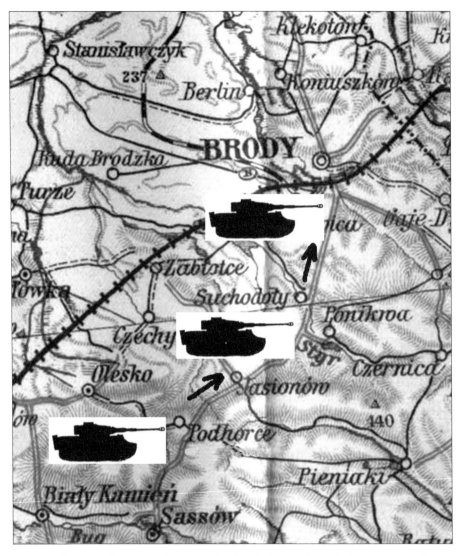

Map showing the route taken by Wirsching's Tigers from Podhorce to Brody.

we bombarded the village, which began to burn brightly. We had achieved our objective and returned to Jezierna where we resumed security duty.

OBERMAYR: First attack on two villages near Jezierna. Battalion commander Major Schmidt accompanied us in our *Schützenpanzerwagen* [SPW, armoured personnel carrier].

24 March 1944

OPERATIONAL ORDERS: '2nd Company, proceed ahead of main battle line east of Ostaszowsce and attack Height 386.'

SEEFRIED: At 0415 hrs, Alarm! The enemy had broken through the southern security and attempted to enter our village. We broke camp and next moment headed for them. The Tigers opened fire to immediate effect. The Russians fled into open country to be mown down by our machine guns [MGs]. A number of them got to houses along the *Rollbahn* but this only served them as a refuge until our quadruple flak arrived. Then we gave pursuit. After they allowed our Tigers to pass by unmolested, there now occurred fierce close-combat clashes with the Russians in the area of our platoon. We dismounted from our SPWs and engaged the enemy with hand grenades and pistols. The Russians defended grimly. One of their hand grenades was lobbed into the SPW of our platoon commander, Leutnant Moser. After the deafening explosion we heard the cries of the wounded. When the rear door opened three men came out, seriously wounded, including Leutnant Moser. The others, Unteroffizier Köple and the radio operator Lang, were dead.

We brought the wounded to the main dressing station by the shortest route and then resumed our security position. We learned that Aigner had also been killed by a bullet to the head.

OBERMAYR: Attack reconnaissance together with 3rd Company at 1700 hrs.

A 507 Battalion Tiger being refuelled from a 200-litre barrel.

25 March 1944

OPERATIONAL ORDERS: '2nd Company, attack on Harbucov and Trestiokizc. 3rd Company, attack on Lopuscany and Troscianiec.'

OBERMAYR: Attack with 3rd Company. Went in the afternoon with Major and Oberstleutnant. Came under heavy mortar fire.

SEEFRIED: Our SPW had engine trouble, we went to the repair yard at Zborov arriving 0900 hrs. It was very cold.

SCHNEIDER: The east has us again! We already have two days of operations behind us. In the first I destroyed two enemy tanks. As to the general situation the weather is vile with snow flurries, mud etc. but that doesn't worry us. The worst is that we never get five minutes for a breather during the day. We leave in the early hours and it is already night when we arrive at some place or other to refuel, load ammunition, clean weapons, check over the vehicle. That generally keeps us busy until midnight. Sentries are then posted. Everybody has to do it, outside or on the turret. If you get three hours' sleep you're lucky!

26 March 1944

OBERMAYR: Radio post with 3rd Company at Oleyov.

SEEFRIED: We left the repair yard and rejoined our platoon towards midday. At 1400 hrs, during a bitingly cold snowstorm, we were ordered to dig in on the hill in front of the railway station so as to observe the enemy's every move 200 m away. An enemy scouting party which appeared suddenly was driven off with MGs. When dusk fell we had expended so much ammunition firing at the station that we needed to bring up a fresh supply. I stood up and a round whistled past my ear. After a second near miss I realised that a sniper had me in his sights. There was nothing for it but to crawl 30 m to the MG. From there we fired back in the direction of the railway station whenever we detected movement. When relieved at 2000 hrs we were frozen stiff and could hardly walk. Back in the village the Russian artillery bombarded us. All hell was let loose! I lay near the SPW gritting my teeth; the shells were falling very close. It lasted about half an hour. Then we returned to our quarters, turned in and slept.

27 March 1944

OPERATIONAL ORDERS: '2nd Company, attack and occupy Szanilovce. 3rd Company, from Oleyov advance to Lopuscany and Hukatovce.'

OBERMAYR: Took a rest.

Officers of 507 in conversation.
From left: Schöck, Wirsching, Berthold and Koltermann.

SEEFRIED: We stood security until evening. The weather has improved.

28 March 1944

SEEFRIED: At 0800 hrs two Tigers and three SPWs, including our vehicle, left on an operation. We had to proceed to the next village, pick up our

General Werner Friebe commanded 8th Panzer Division in 1944.
The mixed battle group bore his surname.

grenadiers and transport them to a position 2 km farther on. We found them waiting and ready for the attack. We drove on, the grenadiers following in line behind us. When the first Tiger reached high ground it came under heavy artillery fire. Four grenadiers were hit by the first burst of shelling, then others fell. We jumped out and brought the seriously wounded into our SPW, a total of six men. This brought the attack to a standstill. We returned to our starting point. The other vehicles also brought in wounded men. Towards 1600 hrs Stukas came over and bombed the railway station. The earth trembled. Nothing there was left alive!

29 March 1944

OPERATIONAL ORDERS: '3rd Company. Advance to Troscianiec and Harbucov.'

SEEFRIED: The front has grown a little quieter. Our Stukas returned at 1000 hrs and bombed Ivan's positions. The weather was glorious, bringing a thaw. We slaughtered a pig and had a feast. At 1500 hrs Bauer received a serious head wound from a single round of mortar fire and collapsed in the dining room. Luckily the medical officer arrived quickly and saved his life. At 2200 hrs we left Jezierna for Brody.

30 March 1944

OPERATIONAL ORDERS: '2nd and 3rd Companies: attack north-eastwards of Dubze and near Ponika.'

SEEFRIED: At 0600 hrs we drove through Zloczov and towards 0930 hrs headed for Brody. We saw the crew abandoning a burning Tiger. Three Ju 88s began a dive; the third machine was hit by anti-aircraft fire and crashed. Ivan was offering stiff resistance. In the evening we found a place to bed down in Dubze. Bobby and I stayed in the quarters while the others stood sentry. I was trying to warm the room when the stove blew up, covering me in ashes. Bobby dragged me away from the wreckage. The incident set light to the whole room and so we grabbed the most essential things and rushed outside. I had a minor head injury but nothing else.

SCHNEIDER: The sixth day of the attack. We stood guard for a bit and I used the time to write a few lines home. Yesterday was my birthday. It did not go off quite as one would have wished: another day of attacks for all of us! We drove into a hole in the snow and it took a lot of laborious effort while under mortar fire to get us free. In the evening, after returning to base, refuelling and re-ammunitioning, the order came to go again. We drove all night until early morning. After a stop to clear the vehicle for action we kept on going. We have occasional sunshine but the weather still leaves a lot to be desired. Now and again we have snow flurries, but sooner or later spring must come, even here!

General Wolfgang Lange, commander of Corps Battalion C, formed from remnants of hard-hit infantry divisions.

General Johannes Nedtwig commanded 545th Security Division, which broke out of the Brody encirclement.

31 March 1944

OPERATIONAL ORDERS: '2nd Company: advance to Hluszyn and clear the *Rollbahn* of enemy from there to Dubze. 3rd Company: advance via Hluszyn to Kazmiry.'

OBERMAYR: We went to 1st Workshop Platoon with engine trouble.

1 April 1944

OPERATIONAL ORDERS: '2nd Company, advance to Hluszyn. 3rd Company, advance to Kazmiry.'

SEEFRIED: Towards 0900 hrs we reached Suchodole and stayed there until 1300 hrs. We were taking our vehicle into the workshop with damage to the gears. On the way we got bogged down in swampy country. A Tiger with damage to tracks and suspension also got stuck 50 m from us. We radioed the recovery platoon: they couldn't tow us out until morning. At that we occupied a house on the *Rollbahn* to spend the night, slaughtered a ram and ate it.

2 April 1944

OPERATIONAL ORDERS: '3rd Company, advance to Hluszyn.'

SCHNEIDER: After the repair staff mended a damaged track, we of Tiger 331 are taking the day off and will probably go forward tomorrow. The Russians are very dogged about getting through to Romania but have suffered very heavy losses. The weather here still has nothing spring-like about it, always these snow flurries and snowstorms against which little progress can be made. My health is first class: many people have not adjusted well to the change of climate but it does not affect me. Yesterday five of us prepared three hens, first boiled and then roasted. Quite excellent!

Major Erich Schmidt, commanding officer, Heavy Panzer Battalion 507.

SEEFRIED: Towards 0900 hrs two recovery platoon tractors arrived and towed us out. After that we headed for Krasne but drove into a ditch at 1700 hrs and stuck fast. In attempting to get free we threw both tracks and in the icy cold it took us some time before we got them fitted again and found quarters in a house.

3 April 1944

OPERATIONAL ORDERS: '2nd Company; advance to Hluszyn.'

SEEFRIED: At 0800 hrs the SS Panzer Division *Hohenstaufen* was unloaded at Krasne and one of their Panzer IVs pulled us out. Next we went to the staff at Zloczov and from there to Lackie where we occupied quarters around 1700 hrs.

4 April 1944

SCHNEIDER: Our Tiger is operational again. The seventh day of attacks is behind us, and I destroyed two more tanks and another two anti-tank guns. It all counts! It is already evening and we are spending the night out here in the field. The wagon is just like a refrigerator. The weather has improved,

A photograph, unfortunately of poor quality, from the first edition of the 507 Battalion journal. *From left to right:* Oberfeldwebel Heinrich Diez, commander of Tiger 331; Unteroffizier Helmut Schneider, gunner; Unteroffizier Kurt Lehmann, driver; Unteroffizier Kurt Kramer, radio operator; Gefreiter Hans Seidl, loader.

yesterday and today we had beaming sunshine. It gives us new hope even if the season of mud has arrived. When we leave the wagon we are up to our ankles in it.

5 April 1944

SEEFRIED: In the afternoon Bobby has to go forward. I am taking over as radio operator.

6 April 1944

SEEFRIED: We have a rest day!

7 April 1944

SEEFRIED: At 0800 hrs I am going to the staff at Zloczov. When I get back to Lackie from there we have to take the wagon to the repair yard. The journey goes through Ocedov to Chvadov.

8 April 1944

SEEFRIED: Over the next four days we will be working on our SPW. The snow has almost melted away. Spring is coming!

13 April 1944

SEEFRIED: We drove to Zborov and from there to Cecova where we spent the night.

14 April 1944

SEEFRIED: At 0700 hrs we went with a Tiger to our readiness area beyond Taurov. The Russian air force is very active.

OBERMAYR: At 1800 hrs went to readiness position forward of a large swamp. Much flak pyrotechnics there.

15 April 1944

ORDERS: '2nd and 3rd Companies: Attack on Chodanczkov-Viyelki.'

SCHNEIDER: During this attack we ran over a mine and had to return to the repair yard with track damage. On the way we came across two hens on which we later dined.

SEEFRIED: At 0900 hrs a major offensive began with the aim of relieving our troops in the Tarnopol encirclement. Enemy aircraft approached repeatedly but always bore away when our flak fired at them. At 1800 hrs we came to a village in flames. After passing through a veritable curtain of fire laid by the Russian artillery we took the village after a bitter struggle. In the night we kept watch over a Tiger stuck in a swamp.

OBERMAYR: Afternoon, advancing towards Tarnopol. Went with Waffen-SS Division *Hohenstaufen* to Kotevska Vilyekce. Heavy artillery fire!

16 April 1944

OBERMAYR: Made further progress towards Tarnopol in company with a Panther battalion. During the fighting, blowout repaired with help of Russian prisoners. War correspondent Zugriegel sat beside me taking photos. We removed the radio equipment from a wrecked T-34.

SEEFRIED: At 0700 hrs special rations, and at 0900 we continued the advance to Tarnopol. Towards 1400 hrs we came under attack from enemy fighter-bombers firing from all barrels. Our fighters shot down two of them. The advance came to a temporary halt when some panzers drove over mines. On this operation we alone took fifty prisoners who had to be 'winkled out' of their holes first.

17 April 1944

OPERATIONAL ORDERS: '2nd Company, advance north of Seredynki.'

SEEFRIED: In the readiness position during the afternoon we received concentrated Russian artillery fire. Then three T-34s suddenly came over the rise about 400m away. I reported this to our commanding officer: when I glanced through the hatch my blood ran cold. The 7.62 cm gun of one of the T-34s was almost lined up on us! But our CO was faster, and his round tore off the turret of the T-34. Immediately afterwards he pounded the other two tanks with his 88 and wiped them out. We cheered like kids! That had been a close shave!

Mixed combat units assembling, probably at Zlocow, in readiness for the thrust aimed at relieving Brody.

OBERMAYR: We made a reconnaissance run to check if the ground will bear the weight of a Tiger. Our counter-shaft broke. At a standstill in the village.

18 April 1944

OBERMAYR: Heavy fire on our village from Russian artillery guns and Stalin organs [Katyusha rocket launchers].

SCHNEIDER: We began the attack to relieve Tarnopol. On the way we ran over another mine. The Tiger didn't even shudder but as we were seated at open hatches around the crew compartment, the enormous explosion set our ears ringing! We repaired the track and after a short while rejoined the pack.

SEEFRIED: The heights this side of Tarnopol cannot be taken! At 1230 hrs we came under deafening and blinding artillery and Stalin organ fire. Sepp and Walter were wounded. We pulled out in the dark. I lost radio contact and had to fire up white flares to get it restored. Some of the Tigers bogged down but could be towed out.

19 April 1944

OBERMAYR: By chance Oberleutnant Steinborn's Workshop Company Tiger came by and towed us free. On the journey through the encirclement the towing hawser broke.

SEEFRIED: We shifted our position but came under heavy artillery fire towards 1700 hrs. At 1900 hrs the operation to relieve Tarnopol continued over Height 386 near Taurov. Here we saw evidence of the bitter fighting, dead of both sides, Russians and men of SS Panzer Division *Hohenstaufen*. In Taurov I was given a job directing traffic.

20 April 1944

SEEFRIED: We went to the repair yard at Zborov and then in the evening to the rest area at Meteniov where we would stay until 30 April. On 22 April I received the Panzer Assault Badge.

OBERMAYR: Our SPW is with the repairs staff.

23 April 1944

OBERMAYR: We drove to the rest area at Meteniov near Zborov.

SCHNEIDER: There is a kind of 'lull before the storm'. We will probably be sent to another hotspot. Our Tiger has already travelled 1,000 km, a remarkable achievement for such a heavy wagon!

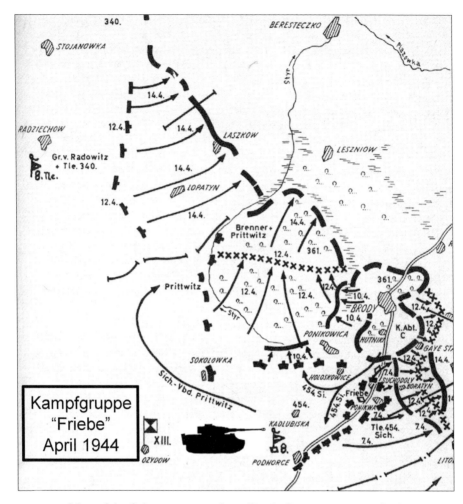

Map of the fighting area involving Battle Group *Friebe*, to which
Panzer Battalion 507 was attached, to relieve Brody in April 1944.

24 April 1944

SCHNEIDER: We are still at the workshop but I will personally not be there
long because I am taking command of my own Tiger. Previously I was gunner
in 331 [= commander's panzer, 3rd Platoon, 3rd Company]. Our commander
was Oberfeldwebel Heinrich Diez, driver Gefreiter Kurt Lehmann, radio
operator Gefreiter Kurt Kramer and loader Hans Seidl.

On 20 April Lehmann was promoted to *Unteroffizier* [corporal] while the
radio operator and loader were both awarded the Panzer Assault Badge in
Silver. That was a pleasant surprise and we took photos straight away.

The same evening I was summoned to rearward services to stand by as
'Commander for special purposes'. I was just making myself comfortable

when told to get ready to lead an anti-partisan group next morning. That was then cancelled because I had to take over a wagon in the workshop. This will be the original wagon of the company commander, 301, which has just been fitted with a new engine. My own crew has been assigned: driver is Panzer-oberschütze Walther from Upper Silesia, radio operator Gefreiter Frischherz from Austria. Rumours suggesting we were going to another sector have been discarded. We are lurking in wait for the enemy tanks which the Russians have got ready in huge numbers between Tarnopol and Brody.

The weather is glorious. The terrain is baked dry and dust lies on the *Rollbahn*. Russia is truly a land of contrasts. Either you bog down in the mud or the dust suffocates you. The fighting here has now become fairly violent. The German public is probably well informed by press and radio about the fighting for Tarnopol and Brody. Many of our fathers fought and bled in this region!

29 April 1944

SCHNEIDER: The company commander, Oberleutnant Neumeyer, handed us the Eastern Front Medal awarded in the summer of 1942.[1] Only the ribbon is to be worn.

1 May 1944

SEEFRIED: We changed location to Podhorce where the battalion will be resting for the whole month. We put up our tents as temporary quarters near the castle. The activity has all quietened down. For the moment we are the 'assault reserve'. In the castle they have arranged a variety show. The weather is still very unstable, hot by day, very cold by night. In the tent we have a decent amount of straw which makes it tolerable.

OBERMAYR: Resting at Podhorce.

3 May 1944

SEEFRIED: I have to attend a radio course until 5 May.

4 May 1944

OBERMAYR: Reconnaissance patrol to Huta-Pieniaka.

8 May 1944

OBERMAYR: Reconnaissance patrol to Zlocov, Zborov and Jezierna.

---

1. Awarded for participation in the 'Winter Battle in the East 1941/1942'.

9 May 1944

SCHNEIDER: Each crew is being allocated quarters. I am with my own crew. In the afternoon we had vehicle inspection. Whoever has served with a motorised unit knows what that means: every screw must be clean, engine and crew compartment shining like the day when they came from the manufacturer, not to mention weapons, ammunition and equipment. Being so close to the front, however, it is not chalked up against you for concentrating only on those items which one knows from experience are important for survival!

Entertainment has also been laid on. I saw the films *Wildvogel* ['Wild Bird'] and *Gefährlicher Frühling* ['Dangerous Spring'], both nice, enjoyable presentations, and also *Feuerzangenbowle* ['Burnt Punch'] with Heinz Rühmann which I had read years before in the book by Spoerl. Naturally in such a rest area there are exercises and weapons inspections, but I don't have to suffer those any more.

10 May 1944

OBERMAYR: Leutnant Moser played Schubert, Bach and Bruckner on the Podhorce church organ, then by agreement ten minutes of Peter Kreuder in return for us working the bellows.

11 May 1944

SCHNEIDER: I have been sent on the course for reserve-officer applicants. From 3rd Company besides myself are one sergeant, a lance-corporal and four privates. When we reported to the commanding officer to sign off, he told us 'veterans' that our next course would be in Germany but the four privates had first to prove their worth at the front. Will I finally get closer to achieving my ambition on this course? We were taken by lorry to the village of Bor a few kilometres south of Podhorce. I was given quarters in a humble cottage.

13 May 1944

OBERMAYR: Reconnaissance patrol with officers near Brody.

14 May 1944

OBERMAYR: Today a promenade concert!

15 May 1944

SCHNEIDER: After three days on the course I had to report back to company. An alarm. This was cancelled and the course continued. Spring has come, the trees are in leaf and the cherry trees in blossom. May beetles drone at dusk and the nights are wonderfully mild.

Propaganda Company images taken at the battle group's readiness position prior to attempting the relief of Tarnopol. An assault gun, a Hummel (Sd.Kfz. 165) self-propelled gun and a 507 Tiger can be seen near various infantry vehicles.

SEEFRIED: We had to parade in the castle park at Podhorce at 1700 hrs. The sun was setting blood red when Feldmarschall Model awarded Major Erich Schmidt the Knight's Cross. Nothing more to report for my part until 1 June.

16 May 1944
SCHNEIDER: I returned to Bor without having attended the Knight's Cross parade the previous day.

18 May 1944
SCHNEIDER: The course was suspended for a second time for another alarm, and again we were soon back at Bor. I think I am doing well on the course. I hope there are no more interruptions in its last four days: apart from the loss of time, driving back and forth along dusty roads is no fun.

21 May 1944
OBERMAYR: Divisional festivities at the Podhorce castle.

22 May 1944
OBERMAYR: We celebrated Leutnant Moser's birthday.

Tiger 331, commanded by Heinrich Diez, with hawser attached prior to being towed.

25 May 1944

SCHNEIDER: The course has finished and I believe that everything has gone well for me. The commandant had criticisms to make about many men (none from 507) and in conclusion said: 'Those whose readiness to be an officer I have adjudged on the basis of course results will be going to the training school very soon.'

26 May 1944

SCHNEIDER: Upon my return to the company I met Heinz Zinke, back from a long spell in the military hospital at Paderborn. Unteroffizier Karl Kerstan has meanwhile been given command of a Tiger.

28 May 1944

SCHNEIDER: It is Whitsun and the finest weather one could hope for. I sunbathed all day and have a good tan. On the second holiday day we had normal duties. This morning we were filmed for the cinema newsreels by propaganda company correspondents. I was playing skat while others chased off the swarms of mayflies. This is the 'honest impression' which the Homeland is given of a soldier's life on the Eastern Front!

31 May 1944

OBERMAYR: Variety evening with fourteen pretty girls.

1 June 1944

SEEFRIED: I have been promoted to Oberschütze.

SCHNEIDER: Having been confirmed as a 'Reserve-Officer Applicant' I am now entitled to wear silver bars on my shoulder straps.

1 June 1944

SCHNEIDER: Sunday! How many have I spent in this enemy land? Sunday is now indistinguishable from any other day. We reserve-officer applicants from 3rd Company were given the 'honourable task' of building a sandbox – in our free time! It's a nice way to keep one busy but makes a lot of work. In a lawn of the local castle park we dug a hole 4 m by 6 m and filled it with yellow sand. Then we had to cut out houses and panzers to put on it and much else. Once it was completed we had Sunday afternoon free. I would like to have sunbathed but the weather turned unfavourable.

6 June 1944

OBERMAYR: We fired live rounds on an exercise.

7 June 1944

SEEFRIED: At 1500 hrs we were relieved by the bridge watch from Plenisko. It is starting up again! Our task: help support the front line north-west of Tarnopol. We set off at 1900 hrs and occupied a readiness position just behind the main front line.

OBERMAYR: In the afternoon we attacked with the Tigers.

8 June 1944

SEEFRIED: The attack began at 0300 hrs. The air was filled with rumbling and rolling thunder. Our artillery batteries fired non-stop. Then our Tigers roared forward, pioneers seated on the hulls.

1000 hrs: Halder and Rühl (both Staff Reconnaissance Company) came back wounded. We captured a Studebaker truck and a 9.2 cm anti-tank gun. Lieck's wagon (Staff Reconnaissance Company) received a direct hit. Haas was killed, the others seriously wounded. Towards 1900 hrs we withdrew, having carried out our mission.

9 June 1944

SCHNEIDER: For three days we have been in action in a peculiar way. It started as an exercise, and then something serious developed out of it, though nothing major. Yesterday I was 'VB' [advanced observer] in the main battle line. I saw some enemy tanks which ran for it as soon as I opened fire at them. The same day we received a hit in the stowage box. Amongst other things, the wonderful windcheater which my mother had sown for me from captured Russian tent material was reduced to ribbons.

OBERMAYR: We joined 3rd Company as radio relay post.

10 June 1944

OBERMAYR: In the evening we returned with 3rd Company. Along the woodside we received heavy fire from anti-tank guns and rifles but suffered no casualties. Rested in Podhorce.

SCHNEIDER: In the afternoon our company commander Fritz Neumeyer received the German Cross in Gold. The 'war' is over and we are back in our old lodgings. Yesterday they held an 'NCOs' evening', starting at 2100 hrs and lasting until seven next morning. The venue was a spooky vault fitted with pitfalls and tripwires.

A 507 Battalion Tiger being loaded with 8.8 cm shells from an armoured personnel carrier. The battalion insignia can be seen at the rear of the Tiger.

On the battlefield at Brody in March/April 1944. In the photo are visible four crew members of Tiger 311 (commander Leutnant Bernd Pfeuffer).

A 507 Battalion Tiger. To the right, a Demag 1-tonne tractor of the repairs unit.

A Tiger being towed out of a morass. Any further attempt to get free
under its own power would only cause the panzer to sink deeper.

Armoured personnel carriers and Tigers, here 212, and Waffen-SS panzer-grenadiers await the order for their battle group to move out.

A 507 Battalion *Gefreiter* (trained private soldier) at the front of a Tiger I.
The plating has evidence of a hit which failed to penetrate.

16 June 1944

SCHNEIDER: After being given the rank of *Fahnenjunker–Unteroffizier* (officer-cadet senior grade) I was despatched to Paderborn with Eribert von Wienskovski. The pay sergeant, Sepp Mayer, let us have a good supply of smokers' requisites for the journey while our company commander gave us a pair of shoulder straps each from his 'collection' as a parting gift.

The shoulder straps remained in Schneider's possession as souvenirs. His service with Panzer Battalion 507 now ended. Upon his arrival at Paderborn as a reserve-officer applicant he was transferred to the panzer-grenadiers as a junior lieutenant, and despite all his efforts never returned to the panzers. Eribert von Wienskovski, in the same group as Schneider at Gross Glienicke, was not commissioned and after the course ended returned to 3rd Company. Nothing is known of his further service or whereabouts. Schneider spent the last months of the war on a Wanderer bicycle. Armed with a Panzerfaust and assault rifle at Oppenheim on the Rhine he faced the advance of the US Army.

19 June 1944

OBERMAYR: Drove to Suchodole with officers. Inspected remote-controlled panzer.

21 June 1944

OBERMAYR: Leutnant Moser is being transferred out.

SEEFRIED: I have been transferred to HQ for a week with the watch commando. Having a good time.

29 June 1944

SEEFRIED: I am back with the battalion. At 1330 hrs we were put on notice to leave for Zloczov where we loaded on rail transports from 1545 hrs. It is said that we are going to the central sector of the Eastern Front. When the train passed through Lemberg many of the men were already drunk.

OBERMAYR: Pulling out of Podhorce. In the afternoon we were loaded at Zloczov. In the evening the train set off in the direction of Lemberg.

Helmut Schneider:
My Experience between Tarnopol and Brody

I wrote the following report on 20 September 1944 at the Senior Cadets School, Gross-Glienicke, Berlin. I beg the reader's indulgence for the rather bombastic style of writing which was expected on the course:

21 March 1944. The onset of spring! Our Tigers were unloaded between Lemberg and Tarnopol. We were full of expectation and hopes regarding the

A Tiger moving out for Operation Hydra. The identity of its commander,
an NCO decorated with the Iron Cross First Class, is not known.

prospects with our fabulous new panzer. The Russians we knew: in the first
year of the Russian campaign we had resisted them victoriously in our light
panzers. We set off without delay, heading for the enemy directly from the
unloading ramp so to speak.

In the spring of 1944 the situation on this sector of the front was very
serious. Our task was to close down a gap in the front 40 km wide. Its ends
were Tarnopol and Brody. For fourteen days we went from one battle to the
next. The struggle against a numerically far superior enemy was not easy, and
what made it especially difficult was the thaw which softened the terrain
everywhere. Many of our panzers suffered mechanical damage, especially to
gears and engines. Thus on Good Friday (7 April) only two Tigers of 3rd
Company were operational, strung out as part of a long line co-operating
with others of 2nd Company to cover an attack by two Panther battalions.
I was gunner in the Tiger of the company commander (Oberleutnant Fritz
Neumeyer). Our companion 3rd Company Tiger was 100 m to our right, its
commander being platoon leader Oberfeldwebel Heinz Diez.

At midday we had just finished off some mixed conserves and were
feeling satisfied and relaxed. In the crew compartment of the panzer it was

icy cold. I had removed my boots and hung them over the cannon, wrapping my feet in blankets. The commander was reading a newspaper, the driver was on watch, radio operator and loader were asleep, understandable after such tension! Suddenly we heard engine noises. Our own panzers were only to our right, in a depression, therefore this must be Ivan!

I had just snatched my boots from the gun when the commander shouted, 'Enemy tanks half right!' The engine started and the turret began to swivel simultaneously. Almost at once I had an enemy tank in the optic, a T-34 moving fast towards our 2nd Company neighbours. Sights 1,000 m, hold steady, fire! Too short! What happened next transpired over a period of six minutes. My second round with sights set for 1,200 m bagged him – a stab of flame showed us that he was done for. Next I saw muzzle flashes to the left. It could not be made out clearly except that the Tigers of our neighbouring company seemed intent on attacking. Our two 3rd Company Tigers moved up and we soon spotted the enemy – five tanks carefully camouflaged in gardens. Because they were all concentrating on the 2nd Company panzers, the Soviets offered us their side profile as a target. The 2nd Company Tigers scored some hits but a number of shells bounced off the Russian armour and so we knew these were heavy tanks we were facing. Soon I could recognise them: heavy self-propelled assault guns. If they manoeuvred to turn those 12.2 cm guns to bear on us we were in trouble. Our commander steered us farther left to make our shooting position more favourable and then we fired round after round. Every round hit! One blast of flame after another showed the effectiveness of our 88. When a couple of Russians attempted to abandon their tank we fired between them with our MG.

It went off better than an exercise with weeks of planning: three assault guns brewed up, and our companion Tiger claimed three T-34s destroyed. Then we came under anti-tank gunfire. Our turret swivelled left. HE rounds, sights 2,200 m – fire! – and an anti-tank gun was no more. The same fate swiftly overwhelmed an anti-aircraft gun in the ground-fire role.

When we took stock, our proud achievement was three heavy assault guns, four T-34s, one anti-tank and one anti-aircraft gun. That had been some six minutes!

In the afternoon when discussing the action with the 2nd Company crews we found that they had received hits but suffered no casualties. But how would it have been if we had not given them such good protection on the flank? Weeks later I saw the photos which radio operator Kurt Kramer had taken secretly from his viewing slit. They created for me an indelible memory of this panzer action in which we two crews of 3rd Company had emerged victorious against nine dangerous opponents.

Richard Durst (Repairs Staff, 3rd Company):
On a 'Sweden Drink' at Podhorce Castle

When we were finally unloaded at Krasne after five days on the train transporter, this did not mean that we had firm ground beneath our feet at last. The ground was unsuitable for the wide and heavy field tracks of the Tigers, not to mention the minefields laid almost everywhere with such cunning. Any modern referee would have declared the pitch unplayable!

Podhorce was the first resting place after the initial weeks of operations of Panzer Battalion 507 in the Tarnopol–Brody area. There followed many fastidious vehicle and weapons inspections, hours set aside for cleaning and repairs, instruction and training, exercising and singing, and naturally doing sentry duty. But we also had off-duty interests: cinema, front welfare, sport and bodily hygiene. Once we even had some Propaganda Company people come to film us 'as we were' hunting down may-beetles (1944 being a major

Tigers of Heavy Panzer Battalion 507 on the move during Operation Hydra, Easter (10 April) 1944.

Leuchtendes Vorbild höchster soldatischer Tugend

Der heldenmütige Kampf der Besatzung von Tarnopol abgeschlossen — Auch die letzten Verteidiger kämpften sich durch

Berlin, 19. April. Nach 25 Tagen erbitterten Ringens hat der heroische Kampf der Besatzung in Tarnopol sein ruhmreiches Ende gefunden, nachdem die letzten Teile der tapferen Verteidiger sich unsere von Westen vorgeschobenen Verbände aufgenommen worden sind. Seit dem Mär haben sich die unter dem Befehl des Generalmajors von Neindorff stehenden deutschen Truppen in der vom Feinde eingeschlossenen Stadt gegen stärkste Kräfteanstrengungen der Sowjets gehalten.

Trotz des verbissenen Widerstandes unserer Grenadiere gewannen die Bolschewisten infolge der zahlenmäßigen und materiellen Überlegenheit von Tag zu Tag mehr Boden. In härtesten Straßen- und Häuserkämpfen schlugen unsere Soldaten die Bolschewisten aber immer wieder zurück. Laufend zugeführte sowjetische Verstärkungen ließen die Lage jedoch immer bedrohlicher werden. Die außerordentlich harten, Tag und Nacht anhaltenden Kämpfe fesselten über sechs Schützendivisionen sowie sehr starke Artillerie- und Panzerkräfte des Feindes, während die geringe Zahl der Verteidiger über keine nennenswerten schweren Waffen verfügte. Vor dem im abnehmenden Artilleriefeuer, das die Stadt ein einziges Ruinenfeld verwandelte, und von ununterbrochenen Angriffen von Tieffliegern und Panzern mühsam unsere Grenadiere schließlich auf den Westrand der Stadt zurückgedrängt. Aber auch hier ließen ihre Gegenstöße

nicht nach, durch die sie feindliche Angriffsgruppen zerschlagen und den Bolschewisten im Nahkampf hohe Verluste zufügten. Nachdem Munitions- und Wassermangel die weitere Verteidigung der Stadt unmöglich gemacht hatte, erging am 15. April der Befehl zum Ausbruch aus der Stadt nach Westen, am gleichen Tage, an dem der Kommandant von Tarnopol, der jetzt mit dem Eichenlaub zum Ritterkreuz des Eisernen Kreuzes ausgezeichnete Generalmajor von Neindorff, inmitten seiner Soldaten den Heldentod fand. Am 16. April traten die noch kampfkräftigen Einheiten in drei Gruppen zum Durchbruch an, um zu den nur noch wenige Kilometer entfernten deutschen Panzerkräften durchzustoßen. Einem Teil gelang dieser Durchbruch bis zum Abend, wobei eine Gruppe noch eine sowjetische Mörserbatterie mit ihrer Bedienung vernichtete. Der Rest schlug sich im Laufe des 17. April durch die sowjetische Linie durch zu der deutschen Panzergruppe, die sich seit Tagen gegen hartnäckigen Widerstand des Feindes und unter den schwierigsten Geländeverhältnissen Schritt für Schritt nach Osten vorgekämpft hatte, um die Männer aus Tarnopol anzunehmen. Diese Panzerkampfgruppe, die sich aus Teilverbänden des Heeres und der Waffen-SS zusammensetzte, hat bei dieser Unternehmung in den letzten drei Tagen 75 Sowjetpanzer, 108 Geschütze sowie zahlreiche Granatwerfer und sonstige Waffen des Feindes vernichtet. Durch das Aus-

harren auf weit vorgeschobenem Posten werden die Tarnopol-Kämpfer für alle Zeiten ein leuchtendes Vorbild höchster soldatischer Tugend sein, ein Vorbild an unübertrefflicher Tapferkeit und unerschütterlicher Standhaftigkeit.

Eichenlaub für einen Sohn der Mark

Aus dem Führerhauptquartier, 19. April. Der Führer verlieh am 13. April das Eichenlaub zum Ritterkreuz des Eisernen Kreuzes an Generalleutnant Johannes Mayer, Kommandeur der rheinisch-westfälischen 329. Infanterie-Division, als 453. Soldaten der deutschen Wehrmacht.

Generalleutnant Mayer wurde am 6. September 1893 als Sohn des Pfarrers M. in Stependit (Westprignitz) geboren.

„Es soll kein Deutschland mehr geben"

Bigo, 19. April. Die Ausrottung nicht nur des Begriffs, sondern auch des Wortes Deutschland ist auf der Teheran-Konferenz beschlossen worden, erklärte Johannes Steel in der Mai-Nummer der Neuyork-Zeitschrift „Clik" in einem „Es wird kein Deutschland mehr geben" betitelten Artikel. Das Blatt veranschaulicht die beabsichtigte Zerstückelung Deutschlands und betont, daß kein einziger der neuen Kleinstaaten irgendeinen Namen tragen dürfe, der noch an Deutschland erinnere. Dieser Beschluß sei in Teheran auf Antrag Stalins gefaßt worden.

'Shining Example of the Highest Soldierly Virtue':
Newspaper report of 19 April 1944 on the final stages of the battle at Tarnopol.

year of infestation apparently), but once the preferred filming nearer the front became more difficult, they quickly withdrew!

Decorations were awarded and promotions handed down. In this connection I mention a company evening which took place in the cellars of Podhorce castle. The cellar was fitted out with pitfalls, tripwire and every possible kind of stuffed animal discovered in the castle. Since promotions had to be celebrated with alcohol, some of the older veterans revived peacetime customs. Stabsfeldwebel Bruno Bethge was probably the initiator of the Sweden Drink which the promoted youngsters were forced to drink, and he emphasised that in former times the drinking vessel had been a sabre scabbard. I had just received my promotion to *Unteroffizier* and with two others, a sergeant and an officer cadet, was forced to partake. The Sweden Drink consisted of high percentage alcohol enriched with all kinds of tasty additives such as pepper, salt and mustard, castor oil and shoe polish. Amazingly the commanding officer of the remote-controlled panzer unit was addicted to it and even took some away with him for later. This company celebration had other consequences which were hard to cover up: Unteroffizier Schwab had a special ration of mustard poured over his black uniform at the field kitchen and Dr Hans Maul probably knew more than he admitted about people shooting out lamps in our quarters with service pistols.

Hubert Hagenberger:
Memories of My First Operations with Tiger 324

It was 24 March 1944. The first night, which we spent at Oleyov, 26 km east of Zloczov, lay behind us. We had parked our Tiger 324 near a house and on firm ground so that in the prevailing temperatures of minus 30° the tracks would not freeze to the soil. Inexperienced and only on operations for a few days, we kept strictly to the instructions laid down by Unteroffizier Anton Henrich, commander of our Tiger, particularly myself as driver. We had noticed a distinct change in him since leaving Wezep in Holland: whereas before this powerful, broad-shouldered man with bushy eyebrows had often been very nervous and prone to fits of temper, now after the first few days on operations he was calmer and even taciturn. Perhaps it had to do with our gunner, Obergefreiter Anton Schuhnort, advising him a week earlier that he should not keep offering me, the driver, advice on how to drive. Whatever the cause, since then there had been a certain tension in the air.

Teams of steppe ponies brought up the necessary spare parts but even these tough animals had difficulty in negotiating the mud.

The crew had been thrown together in Holland. The small Smerling, always with a smile on his lips, was loader: Franz Lehenbauer, who came from my region, was radio operator. We interacted quite well: everybody knew his job but, despite that, the shortcomings resulting from too short a period of training began to manifest themselves in the first days of operations.

We were heading towards the enemy. After a heavy snowstorm cleared we suddenly had before us some Russian tanks which we engaged immediately. The last of them fell victim to a barrage of fire under the leadership of the company commander. After that it all fell quiet on the enemy side, just two heaps of mangled steel. When we were pushing forward across the plain next day, Ivan raked us with artillery fire which began to come ever closer. I was not aware that we were carrying infantry on the hull because Henrich failed to inform me when we made a short stop in the village. Our attack petered out. I put the engine into neutral, selected the fourth reverse gear and awaited the order to reverse. Meanwhile Ivan's guns had got our range and his shells were falling all around us.

I heard the expected order in my earphones and my pressure on the starter button wiped out two German soldiers. The panzer bobbed slightly and then burrowed back into the snow. I saw before us our tracks in the snow then a pair of boots and a kind of small suitcase. 'Driver halt!' I heard the order ring in my ears and then there was a deathly silence.

'Franz,' I asked the radio operator, 'what is that case ahead?' He fired a brief burst with his MG and the suitcase blew up. It probably contained hand grenades. Now I heard in the earphones, 'Man, those poor boys, we've run over two of them.' I couldn't fully grasp what had happened. The horror of it choked me. The attack continued. Later we established the tragic details. The infantry with us had taken cover from the artillery fire behind the panzer, and failed to react quickly enough when I reversed.

As we proceeded, the snow began to obscure my viewing slit and I cleared it away with my boots. We entered a village whose cottages were taken under fire from three sides. The effect was enormous. Russian troops poured out from every door and window and took to their heels eastwards up a hill. The brown-clad figures were easy to pick out against the snow. Under our MG fire only a few had a chance to escape alive. Finally all movement in the snow stopped, the attack was called off and we rolled back to Oleyov.

I parked the Tiger and bedded it on straw in front of our quarters. I could see strips of flesh in the tracks, a ghastly sight. We asked some of the infantry-men about the unfortunate victims: they were a nineteen-year-old and a family man from the Sudetenland. We went into our lodgings depressed and sad. The owners of the cottage stared at us anxiously. These poor people, once subjects of the Austro-Hungarian monarchy, now faced an uncertain future. Many of the older folk spoke German and one of them had once been in the Austrian Army in quarters at Eferding near Linz. We had no time to reflect on all this. Those not given sentry duty sank exhausted into the straw, to arise next morning ready to face the awful present.

At sunrise I climbed over the iced-up tracks into the panzer, dropped into the driver's seat and let the engine warm up. Then I rolled the machine back and forward a little to check the suspension. Oil pressure was good, everything in order and next I checked the track bolts. The morning was icy cold.

The cottages of Oleyov, simple structures of wood and clay under a roof of straw, trembled as four Tigers roared in from the east one after the other, one of them with a Russian anti-tank gun in tow. Leutnant Berni Pfeuffer, whom I knew from Cherkasy, climbed out happily and described his assault on an enemy anti-tank gun position. Everybody admired his bravado, particularly since he had brought along the gun to prove it. So this was one of the things which made life so difficult for us. Little did we know that in the afternoon a 'Pak' [*Panzerabwehrkanone*, anti-tank gun] like that would bring us death and destruction.

'*Panzer marsch!*' ordered Unteroffizier Anton Henrich and our 324 pulled out as the second and not fourth panzer of 2nd Platoon, 3rd Company, following platoon commander Leutnant Eychmüller. The other two panzers were non-operational, one being in the workshop and the engine of the other had overheated as soon it started up. Its driver, Kugler, was fiddling about under the engine cover embraced by fumes and smoke. This meant that only two Tigers were heading to Bialoglovy on a difficult mission. The journey took us uphill, past a church with a large onion dome, then into open country where we soon came to the main battle line, hardly recognisable as such. There lay our infantry in hollows in the ground, trembling with cold, bedded on straw but without shelter or cover. Some of these 'warriors' had been brought into our village in the early hours, boys with frozen feet!

An infantry colonel climbed into Eychmüller's panzer while we received a junior lieutenant. The officers were curious to witness a panzer attack at first hand. Ahead of us lay rolling hills, still deeply covered in snow. The two Tigers pushed forward slowly, first through bushy terrain, 324 to the left climbing a low hill, Eychmüller with driver Josef Placzek descending slightly into a valley. It was quiet, no Russian could be seen. About 1,000 m ahead of us was a ridge with a copse of pine trees. From there Henrich suddenly saw the muzzle flash of a Pak. 'Advance to the next hill!' he ordered.

324 roared through the deep snow, engine howling. When we reached the crest and Henrich ordered 'Halt!' the Tiger see-sawed. We had been served

up as if on a plate in full view of the enemy. Russian infantry were nearby. We had scarcely fired our first round than the Russian Pak fired its second round and hit our tracks right side.

Henrich's order 'Driver go back!', which would have brought us into a kind of more favourable reverse-slope position, came too late and now we began receiving hits from everywhere, luckily none of them armour-piercing. As our panzer rolled back, to my horror I saw the right track stretching out in the snow. I reported this to Henrich who seemed very excited and in a hoarse voice ordered me to bring the panzer down into the gulley. Having shed its right track, however, the panzer sagged to the right while the left track turned us in a circle.

'Out!' I shouted, but nobody reacted. When I looked behind me next I saw that the crew compartment was no longer occupied but that the turret

A peculiarity of Heavy Panzer Battalion 507 was that the panzer's number was also painted on the spare track segments attached to the turret which often obscured the one on the hull. The first numeral of the three-figure number was always large and stood for the company: the second numeral indicated the platoon and the third the number of the panzer within the platoon.

This Tiger was driven up a soft slope but failed to make it. An 18-tonne tractor is attempting to stabilise the panzer.

was still turning. I switched off the engine. I noticed that the emergency exit hatch was open. When I removed my earphones I heard for the first time what was happening around me. Nothing! Now I was seized by panic, the only thing that mattered was to get out! I opened the driver's hatch, the Russians fired and hit it. I locked it shut, noticing radio operator Franz Lehenbauer wriggling into the turret with a smoke candle.

'I can't get us away from here,' I told him, 'we've lost the right track.'

'We'll make smoke,' he replied. I thought this was a good idea to cover our escape but searched in vain around the turret base for the igniter. Now we had no option but to evacuate the panzer at once and I dived headlong through the emergency exit into the open, making a soft landing in the deep snow by the wheels. I saw Eychmüller's Tiger standing in a depression about 150 m away;

two men clad in black lay on the ground motionless between our two panzers.

For me there now began a race with death. What we had been taught in training I now had to put into practice: jump up, run, run, lie down, roll to one side, jump up again, run, run! Without gloves I was suffering terribly with the cold. In a depression in the ground I spotted the wreck of a Soviet tank which seemed to offer good cover. I reached it breathless. Until then, Ivan had even been firing at me with armour-piercing shells. Looking cautiously beyond the steel colossus I saw two grey figures with pointed caps creeping up stealthily. Without any kind of weapon I had no chance. I thought of home and decided that it ended here.

Suddenly I heard the noise of an approaching panzer. Here was my last chance! First I saw the rod aerial appear, then I waited at the edge of the earth bank until the panzer was close enough and then, with a couple of leaps and bounds I was in front of the Tiger waving to its driver, Placzek. He opened the hatch cover – in an instant I was inside the panzer and slid behind the driver into the crew compartment, fighting for breath like a hunted wild animal. By loader Hans Zauner stood the infantry colonel who, like the lieutenant with us in 324, had wanted to experience an attack at first hand. Eychmüller gave me a cigarette and his panzer set off again.

On its turret lay Franz Lehenbauer, still alive, and the infantry lieutenant in a winter camouflage suit wheezing from a chest wound. He had not been able to climb and the brave little Smerling had helped him up on the panzer. That had cost Smerling his life. Franz said he had been shot in the head. Our commander Anton Henrich had been killed while abandoning 324. Gunlayer Anton Schuhnort was hit between the two panzers.

'You two bring the lieutenant to the main battle line and stay with him until help arrives!' was the order we survivors of 324 were given as we dismounted. The lieutenant could hardly stand and when we delivered him to his unit he collapsed almost lifeless into their arms. Behind us Eychmüller's 88 suddenly thundered and finished off 324, around which the Russians were already gathering. On the way back when we passed the church where our attack had begun, Franz said, 'Now I'm a believer again somewhat!'

'Surviving crew of wagon 324 reporting back,' I informed Oberleutnant Fritz Neumeyer and *Spiess* (Battalion sergeant-major) Ignatz Bäumler on our return. They merely stared and after a few questions we were dismissed. A year later I met Anton Schuhnort at the Fallingbostel training depot. After escaping from 324 he had been wounded by MG fire in the neck and arms and had collapsed unconscious. When 324's turret fell off it woke him and he waited until dusk before making it back to our lines. We had reported him dead!

Franz Lehenbauer and I were allocated a fresh billet. We were driven to the church at Zloczov, which was still adorned by the five-pointed red star of the Soviet Union. Probably nobody had had the time to take it down. Our hostess, an old *babushka*, blubbered when she saw me and lamented for her child, who was my age, and stroked my cheeks. I was ashamed that I found a mother's distress irritating. Her son was probably a soldier or partisan somewhere; it was difficult for anybody to know what was going on in Galicia.

It was a bright moonlit night as I stood my turn as sentry. I saw a figure dart into a barn. I advanced, which was imprudent, and heard a rustling in the straw. Nobody obeyed my order to come out! I was doubtful about shooting and so just kept my eye on it from a nearby haystack. Perhaps it was 'Malinki' the landlady. Once my relief came I spent the rest of the night on an old sofa in Zloczov.

Hubert Hagenberger (final rank *Gefreiter*): My Memory of Operation Tarnopol

After we had had 324 shot out from under us on 24 March 1944 I was put into the rear echelon at Zloczov and was present when they discussed my next posting. Leutnant Bernhard Pfeuffer, a hefty Nuremberger with whom I had served at Cherkasy, wanted me as his driver. The commander of 3rd Platoon, Oberfeldwebel Heinz Diez, was also in the market when Stabsfeldwebel Bruno Bethge ruled, 'I'll take him. You youngsters all fall out.' Bethge was apparently a man who commanded respect even if, as in this case, he had a very unmilitary manner. Pfeuffer accepted it, however, and naturally my own opinion was not consulted. With a smart '*Jawohl*' I marched out under the gaze, through gold-rimmed spectacles, of 3rd Company Commander, Oberleutnant Fritz Neumeyer.

I introduced myself immediately to the crew of my new Tiger, 313, to which Bethge had appointed me as driver. Gunner was Hofmann from Bad Kissingen, radio operator Joachim Moje from Leipzig and loader Franz Pass from Lower Austria. While the panzer was still at the workshop we were housed in a wooden shack and slept on a bed of straw on the floor at night. Franz Pass had 'organised' farm produce from the locals and Bethge was very complimentary about his brave loader's home-brewed egg flip. One day watched by Neumeyer (and probably with his approval) at long range with a 98k carbine Franz killed a hare hopping across ploughed land. It did not surprise us to learn that he had 'hunted a bit' in the past.

At the workshop I made the suggestion that a segment of track could be fitted to the front of the panzer not only as a spare but also for additional armour

During a road journey, Tiger 321 collapsed a bridge. The problem is now to retrieve the 60-tonne panzer from the river.

protection. This suggestion was not only accepted but fitted immediately to all the battalion's panzers.

On 14 April 1944 we were given notice of a very important operation for this sector, the relief of Tarnopol. At Taurov on the way to Horodyce, and farther on towards Stobotka, we received artillery fire. The bridge over the Wozucka was still being constructed by the pioneers and so we had to wait in open country. Through my viewing slit I saw Oberleutnant Wirsching, 2nd Platoon Commander, going from panzer to panzer, probably to pass instructions to each commander. He did this with surprising imperturbability, disappearing occasionally behind great fountains of earth and dirt. We had scarcely received the warning of mines when Wirsching's panzer, ahead to our left, was suddenly enveloped in smoke, having apparently run over one. Finally the new bridge was ready. Under the great weight of each Tiger it adopted an alarming angle of tilt every time but survived. On the other bank was a fairly steep slope where numerous panzers and SPWs of SS

Photo taken by Helmut Küssner in August 1944 showing his predecessor as
Chief of the Workshop Company, Oberleutnant Schmidt, seated on the bonnet
of a VW Schwimmwagen with a 'damaged' Tiger 'in tow'.

Panzer Division *Hohenstaufen* had assembled. We were attacked by a *Rata*
[Polikarpov I-16 fighter]: somebody placed an MG on Placzek's shoulder and
after a few rounds the aircraft departed, never to return, giving us the chance
to sort ourselves out without Ivan watching from above.

We set off. Reaching the crest of a hill we came under heavy artillery fire
but hardly any other opposition. We overran their artillery position in the
next village, but 313 was far out on the right flank and took no part. Along
the railway line 313 was mined, leaving the left track stretched out on the
grass amongst the primroses. The railway embankment had been secured by
the Waffen-SS for some time, but after the entire force moved forward we
were left to our own devices.

These two crewmen are unidentified. Obviously the Schwimmwagen could not
move a Tiger an inch.

About a kilometre away on the far side of the embankment was a small wood with a much larger one to its right. Left of them both an onion-shaped church tower peered. Before our eyes a swarm of Ilyushin-2 fighter-bombers destroyed the Stanislau–Tarnopol railway line: one of these aircraft headed directly towards us but then dropped his bomb on the permanent way, leaving the ends of the rails reared up vertically.

'Open all hatches and lower the gun barrel,' Bethge ordered. 'It's best we play dead until we fit the track on again.'

The noise of the battle for Tarnopol could be heard to the east. I jumped down and saw that the track was so far behind the panzer that the thin hawser wouldn't reach it, therefore we had to remove segments from the track for reassembly where we were stranded. This kept everybody busy for some time. The mine explosion had deformed the drive sprocket into a slightly oval shape and thirteen track members were no longer usable. Luckily we had enough

Men of the Workshop Company during a break near their Henschel lorry. The letter 'J' stands for 'Instandsetzung' – repairs unit. Unfortunately the photograph has been damaged over the years.

in reserve. Meanwhile Bethge had been observing the woods and established that the enemy had been infiltrating the larger wood without let-up, and so we increased our efforts to the maximum.

That beautifully warm spring day had been the last for one of the soldiers lying on the railway embankment. When I removed his damaged steel helmet I read his name. Horst had been just nineteen. We might have been able to help another soldier beyond the embankment in a field of green corn. With binoculars Bethge could not make out it if was one of our infantry or a Russian. I heard his dreadful cries in my ears long afterwards. They sounded more Russian than German and his uniform looked more like one of theirs. He was lying unfavourably positioned between ourselves and the woods, therefore in the field of fire of both sides and so nobody dared go to his aid. This war was ruthless, with neither space nor time for humanity.

At last we got the track laid out for the panzer wheels to roll over. We had to dig out a metre at the end of the track before we could hammer home the last bolt. Without our knowledge, a German Nebelwerfer unit had moved up 2 km to our rear and suddenly their rockets came howling past overhead to fall in the woods where the Russians had formed up to attack our flank. We had fixed the track without any attention from the enemy but when we went into the village members of a Russian battalion were there to fetch water and chased us over the fields like hares.

Our midday meal was rolled barley heated with a blow lamp. Naturally we might have had something better but Papa Bethge was saving it. The Schokakola chocolate drink had long since been used up and the tins refilled with ballast: at the inventory of rations the controllers were satisfied if the contents of the tin felt the right weight.

Tarnopol had been relieved. Some figures appeared from the town, probably the first to break out of the encirclement. No longer soldiers, most of them unarmed, their features marked by tension and struggle, in their torn and tattered rags they looked like refugees. Pale and famished they tottered over the ploughed meadows of flowers towards a fresh uncertainty.

313 was ready to roll but our mission now was to secure the area against Russian attacks. That night on sentry duty I was even issued with a machine pistol and flare gun. Towards midnight when something white came towards me from the railway embankment I fired a flare to see it better. Unfortunately I was standing close to the panzer and my elbow struck it hard with the recoil. This put me out of action for a while and with one arm hanging down I finally made out what was approaching – a cow loaded with bedding accompanied by a man and woman. Were they really fugitives or spies coming to assess the situation? I accosted this strange party. In response to my question they

pointed to the west and said, '*Na domoi*' ('Going home'). I let them pass. There were so many fugitives in those days.

Next day panzers drove back with infantry riding on the hulls or followed by prisoners. 313 had thirty-five men aboard and we high-tailed it out of there. For us Operation Tarnopol was over.

Dr Max Wirsching (final rank *Hauptmann*): Special Operation Brody, Spring 1944

Brody in Polish Galicia, a town near the northern source of the Bug River, was surrounded. Inside it were 800 seriously wounded German troops trapped without medical supplies or provisions. Several attempts had been made by the Waffen-SS (Divisions *Hohenstaufen*, *Frundsberg*) to relieve the town or at least send in help for the wounded but all had been unsuccessful.

A possible umbilical cord was the road between Podhorce and Brody. Though open, it was mined and in general the Russians kept an eye on mine barriers! The mission received by the commanding officer of 507 Panzer Battalion, presumably from Generalmajor Friebe, required that a convoy of supply vehicles, supported by Tiger tanks, would proceed from Podhorce to Brody in order to supply the 800 wounded soldiers trapped in the encirclement. For this probable 'suicide mission' Major Schmidt appealed to the platoon leaders for a volunteer to lead the operation, and let it be understood that this operation, the success of which would save the lives of numerous German soldiers, would merit the Knight's Cross. Despite that nobody came forward, and so Major Schmidt stated that he was obliged to appoint somebody and his choice fell on Oberleutnant Wirsching as the oldest and probably most experienced officer. Wirsching insisted that every panzer crew member must be a volunteer, and as a result it was mainly men of his own platoon and 2nd Company who manned the Tigers protecting the convoy.

Attached to this convoy would also be one platoon of pioneers, and several SPWs with panzer-grenadiers and medical teams. Five Tigers would form the spearhead, a sixth the rearguard, and between these panzers would be around eighty lorries and the SPWs. The journey according to the map was 12.5 km. All drivers had to keep an eye on their mileage indicator and so remain aware of how far it was to the objective.

The convoy left at dusk. Hauptfeldwebel Hugo Arnold's leading panzer was the first to run over a mine. The crew transferred to an SPW which continued on towards Brody. Wirsching's Tiger was the second to be disabled by a mine; Wirsching and his radio operator transferred to the third Tiger, and this was repeated three more times until he got to Brody in the rearguard

Hauptmann Maximilian Wirsching was awarded the Knight's Cross on
7 February 1945 as commander of 2nd Company, Panzer Battalion 507.

Tiger which had been called forward. Upon arrival, the town commandant, a
one-armed general, embraced him.

Wirsching wrote in a letter to Schneider later:

'I have explained how we overcame the enemy resistance including by the use of our disabled panzers. We saw a light 300 m left of us and fired at it with armour-piercing shells. We hit a structure, apparently a barn, which burst into flame and illuminated the battlefield for us. Each of the commands I transferred to was mined. I had no contact with company, battalion or division and finally when I had to bring up the last Tiger from the rearguard I was doubtful if there was any point in going on, for if we lost the sixth and last Tiger we would have "had it". Thinking of the 800 wounded men was decisive, quite apart from the fact that the lorries would not have been able to turn back even after the pioneers had cleared the minefields.'

Wirsching also recalled that one of his Tiger drivers, who sustained a serious leg injury in a mine explosion, was taken back in a motorcycle sidecar. He himself was deaf for weeks due to the explosions.

Surprisingly this special operation was forgotten until 1985 when, besides Max Wirsching and Hugo Arnold, other men present, Helmut Gutmann (driver), Willi Wolf (commander), Johann Steyskal (radio operator) and Rudolf Pointer (loader) all gave their accounts of it. Max Wirsching was not awarded the Knight's Cross hinted at for this operation, although he received it in 1945 for other reasons. Probably someone else had 'a prior claim'. Soon after the relief of Brody he received other honours such as the German Army Honour Roll Clasp[1] and a mention in the *Wehrmacht Bulletin*.

Helmut Küssner:
From the Everyday Life of the Workshop Company

Helmut Küssner was chief of the workshop at the time when 507 was being formed and recalled the following:

The CO had promised panzer drivers that those whose Tigers went 2,000 km without requiring a change of engine would receive a long special leave. This led to the following interesting case. A Tiger, whose number I cannot remember, was brought into the workshop with the complaint that the engine stuttered when running. On the test stand, however, it ran perfectly. Because the fighting unit was not in action, we could search for the cause with due

---

1. The Ehrenblattspange des Heeres was awarded 'for having performed an act of bravery above and beyond the call of duty that did not justify the Knight's Cross of the Iron Cross and had not been rewarded with the German Cross in Gold'.

Helmut Küssner in civilian clothing at the start of his military service at Goldap in East Prussia.

Helmut Küssner as an *Unteroffizier* in Infantry Regiment 22 stationed at Goldap.

Helmut Küssner (seated right) as a *Gefreiter* with Infantry Regiment 22.

Helmut Küssner also became a driving instructor and is seen here supervising learner drivers on the Demag one-tonne tractor.

diligence. Trial runs brought the same result, therefore it could only be the fuel supply. So we exchanged carburettor, filter, fuel lines and finally the entire engine. Nothing made it any better. This meant that the problem must be the fuel tank.

We discovered that the Tiger had received a hit on the rear side which had dented the hull and the fuel tank. Parts of the tank's inner layers had flaked off and settled at the bottom. On the move, these flakes continually obstructed the filter of the drain pipe and disturbed the uniform flow of the fuel. We changed the tank, put back the old engine and a short time afterwards the driver was awarded his well-deserved special leave.

The number of panzer drivers who achieved this desirable goal was surprisingly high – I think it was seventeen! In order to speed up repair times for Tigers and release technical staff for more complicated repairs I selected fifteen men with technical qualifications from amongst the Russian prisoners brought in by our battalion, and these men were put to work on tracks and suspensions with an interpreter. The unit was led by an Obergefreiter from Poland who oversaw the work. These Russians were very hard workers and so

Helmut Küssner was particularly interested in mechanical engineering and therefore chose the career of an army technical officer. He is seen here at the drawing board during his studies.

were well paid and fed. When the retreat crossed the German border we had to hand these *Hiwis* over to a PoW camp.

Helmut Küssner (*second from right*) with other trainees in the motor shop.

Rudi Beilfuss, initially a platoon commander in 1st Company, recalled the first operations of the company:

During the work in the spring of 1944 in Galicia, 1st Company fought until 30 April at Kowel in terrain unsuitable for heavy panzers. For this reason, the Commander-in-Chief, Fourth Army, Generaloberst Erhard Raus, released the company to battalion. After the situation around Tarnopol and Brody stabilised, 1st Company was assigned to 8th Panzer Division under Generalmajor Friebe.

Gerd Eychmüller: The Art of Baling out from a Panzer

Gerd Eychmüller, already mentioned in Hubert Hagenberger's report, recalls one of seven missions in which he took part in the Tarnopol/Brody area as follows:

As commander of 2nd Platoon, 3rd Company, my crew being Placzek (driver), Engelhardt (gunner), Zauner (loader) and Graf (radio operator), we were part of a large troop unit led by panzers and followed by infantry in SPWs. Making an attack, we passed a village on our right. At its edge we observed that the Russians had dug in Paks. One of them fired and hit our fine, previously undamaged Tiger on the left side, the shell passing through the bodywork, igniting powder spilled from a damaged shell and tearing away the see-saw pedals for the turret rotating mechanism beneath the feet of the gunner. A few seconds later Engelhardt, his feet burning hot, was sitting on my lap. Driver and loader had left the panzer through their individual hatches without difficulty, but the gunner and I found it more difficult because the turret entrance was not designed for two men to pass through at the same time, one wearing a pistol whose holster was fixed very firmly to a broad belt. Nevertheless, the flames were now such that a way was found and we got to freedom together though the pistol holster tore off.

The situation for the radio operator, whose hatch would not open, looked hopeless because the gun was at the 'one-thirty position'. This angle of traverse was unfavourable if one was receiving Pak fire from the left for then the whole linkage gear stood behind the radio operator's seat so that he had no access into the turret. Fortunately Graf was slim and the temperature so hot that the impossible was achieved and after a short time we four who had already bailed out of the panzer could greet our fifth man joyfully. We had all been more or less 'singed' and were picked up by one of the SPWs behind us.

Siegfried Beck:
In Memoriam Leutnant Berni Pfeuffer, and 'Viktor's story'

When we were then Panzer Battalion 507 (Tigers), I was the driver of 311 which was the platoon commander's panzer of 1st Platoon, 3rd Company. Our commander was Leutnant Bernhard Pfeuffer, gunner Paule, loader

Moje, radio operator Schreckenstein. In our baptism of fire in Galicia, a T-34 shot away a track cover. We were spearhead panzer, and as we neared a village held by the enemy I noticed a Pak, but my warning shouts were drowned by Leutnant Pfeuffer: 'Go over the *Holmen!*' [*Holmen* = beams or spars]. I was already in forward sixth gear but what did I know about *Holmen*? I crushed the Pak starting from the muzzle. Luckily our tracks remained intact.

Leutnant Pfeuffer was a very daredevil type. I remember on an attack as I was about to run over some civilians lying on the ground and whom I had

Helmut Küssner (*right*) in the winter of 1936–7 on an exercise at the
Troop Training Depot, Arys.

Helmut Küssner's hard work was rewarded with successive promotions. he is seen here as an *Oberfeldwebel* in Vienna, August 1943.

Helmut Küssner as an *Oberleutnant (Ing.)* commanding the Workshop Company of Heavy Panzer Battalion 507, summer 1944.

taken for enemy close-combat troops or partisans, he stopped me. I had just shortly before received a hit to the viewing slit shield from an anti-tank rifle.

On the operations to break the Tarnopol encirclement, 314 drove through a minefield. I saw the traces ahead left by a Russian tank and was pleased to have found a way through but hit a mine all the same! We received a Pak hit simultaneously in the right drive sprocket where the shell came to rest. In order to get the panzer mobile again we had to insert some replacement segments into the damaged track – while under fire! For this purpose we enlisted the services of some prisoners who had been brought in shortly before. Amongst them was Viktor, who was from Moscow and had been a member of the Pak gun crew which had probably fired the shell to do the damage. The gear rim of the drive wheel was so badly damaged that we had no option but to return to the repair staff workshop.

Workshop Company personnel overhauling the engine from a Tiger in need of a general refit.

As we were crossing a river we nearly overturned on the bridge when the subsoil shifted. On our way back, Viktor sat forward with me on the hatch lighting my cigarettes. At a stop I was about to jump down from the bow of the panzer but Viktor held me back, pointing to a 'coffin mine' lying directly below. It was dug in and the part of it which remained visible looked like a piece of wood. I expressed my gratitude to Viktor for saving my life by letting him change the engine oil when we got back to base. To do that the ground plate had to be unscrewed in order to open the oil drainage screw. This was a filthy job because the oil would first of all run down your sleeve. Therefore

while Viktor was busy changing the oil I went off to the kitchen to get us both a meal. When I came back Oberleutnant Neumeyer, the Company Commander, was standing by my panzer, mesmerised by the pair of Russian boots projecting from underneath the hull. When he heard the story he put Viktor on the fuel detail and not into a PoW camp.

Heinz Stracke (radio operator, final rank *Gefreiter*): Rest Days at Podhorce

Coming from Paderborn, I arrived at Podhorce, Galicia, where 3rd Company was resting after its first operation in the Tarnopol–Brody area. In the castle, little involved in the war, were located the battalion staff and elements of 3rd Company. The Tigers were parked well camouflaged. By the wall of the castle garden, in the shadow of old trees, was the 3rd Company field kitchen whose cooks made sure we were well fed during the R&R. As a newcomer I lived with a crowd of other company members in a large house along the main road where we made the occasional effort to cook for ourselves. In those days I would receive from home a parcel containing amongst other things items much sought after by the local civilian population and which were therefore suitable for barter.

A driver from the support platoons whose name I do not recall was a skilled 'negotiator' to whom I entrusted a number of 'articles'. In exchange for combs, flints, earrings and rosaries he would bring us eggs and bacon. Since we had numerous Austrians, particularly Viennese, in the company, pancakes were also much favoured for which the cook would sometimes add seasoning and a garnish.

Many black birds flew around the massive square castle tower. These were identified by the ornithologists amongst us as jackdaws. One day in the castle park we found a young bird which we picked up and fed, initially with pre-chewed bread, but later he did it himself. 'Jacob', as we christened him, could fly but never left us. Often he would be out of sight but when we called he would come fluttering over with a loud caw. After a while he could even repeat his name and so the small black ball of feathers gave us much pleasure.

At the end of June 1944 the rest period at Podhorce came to an end. We were loaded up and when the heavily laden tank transporter train headed to the west, the glad word was 'Western Front'. But it did not turn out like that!

Hubert Hagenberger: From Podhorce to Baranovicze

The great departure from the so-familiar Podhorce began on 29 June 1944. We trundled through Sassov and Zloczov to the marshalling yard where the transporter trains awaited. That night we were bothered constantly by those nuisances the 'Duty NCOs' [Russian light bomber aircraft]. We awoke to a glorious summer's day and the train went via Rava-Russkaya to Lublin which, with its pointed spires and huge water towers, provided a wonderful picture of peace in the hinterland of the approaching front.

We stopped just outside Lublin alongside a hospital train on the neighbouring track. The soldiers in the cattle trucks made a pitiful sight in their cut-open uniforms with bloodied bandages on all possible parts of the body. 'This is what's in store for you!' one of the patients shouted over, which made us all feel uneasy. Who would want to finish up like that? At least they had the advantage of coming away from the front.

Our train continued into the warm summer's evening and soon the stars were twinkling high above us. The rumours were doing the rounds that we were bound for the invasion front in the West, but when the train stopped near Sielce I looked for the Pole star, and as the train set off again, I could advise my fellow travellers that we were heading east.

It is difficult to describe the disappointment. Everybody had been hoping for a 'more pleasant' enemy in the West! On 2 July 1944 we crossed the River Bug at Brest Litovsk. It was spanned by a huge steel bridge which I photographed as we crossed. On the morning of 3 July we could make out a pair of silvery glinting radio masts on the eastern horizon. After searching my memory I was able to inform everybody that we were at Baranovicze. Towards midday we arrived there and alighted from our rolling transporter under the protection of a quadruple flak gun.

Frontal view of Tiger 114, having shed a track on a muddy unmade track.
The recovery crew now have the laborious task of fitting another. Filthy work!

Tiger 114 seen from the rear. The hull has been raised for the removal of earth.

Left: Helmut Küssner (*left in photo*) with members of his recovery squad taking a break during repairs to Tiger 114 at Podkomien on 20 April 1944.
Below left, below & overleaf: A series of photos from the workshop compound at Zichenau in the autumn of 1944.
Below left: A mobile Strabo crane able to lift 126 tonnes has removed the turret of a Tiger. The drive and running wheels lie strewn about.
Nearer the camera is Tiger 132 resting on segments of its own tracks.

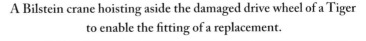

A Bilstein crane hoisting aside the damaged drive wheel of a Tiger
to enable the fitting of a replacement.

Series of photos showing Tiger 113 with a Bilstein crane on a lorry chassis.
Two men are working in the empty engine compartment of the panzer.

Side view of Tiger 132. To the left work is proceeding on a Tiger hull.
A third Tiger can be seen between the two in the background.

View from Tiger 113 over the swivelling Bilstein crane (1.5 tonnes lifting capability) mounted on a lorry platform. The two men working in the empty engine compartment are presumably making ready for the reinstallation of the engine.

This series of three photos shows Tiger 221 having to be towed out of a gully after breaking through a wooden bridge.

The towing hawser has been attached and cautious attempts made to haul the Tiger up.

Side view of Tiger 221. Many Russian bridges were unable to support a vehicle weighing over 60 tonnes.

Chapter 4

FROM BARANOVICZE TO SCHARFENWIESE

On 22 June 1944, the third anniversary of the beginning of the campaign in the East, the Russians launched an offensive with 140 infantry divisions and 43 tank groups. Army Group Centre, against which it was unleashed, was holding 1,000 km of front line with just 34 infantry divisions, 18th and 25th Panzer-Grenadier Divisions and 20th Panzer Division. The front collapsed and the enemy armour and masses of infantry headed westwards unstoppably towards Minsk. Comprehensive destruction of railways by partisans prevented German reserves being brought up in time.

In the wake of these events in the central sector, Panzer Battalion 507 was transferred to the area around Baranovicze. On 5 July 1944, Fourth Army

A destroyed German field howitzer position. Attempts often had to be made to counter Russian tank attacks by the use of flat-trajectory artillery fire.

Russian infantry advancing in the Carpathians, August 1944.

was overwhelmed, Ninth Army forced back to Baranovicze and Third Army to the Lithuanian border. Contact with Army Group North was lost and new Russian offensives began simultaneously against Army Groups North and South. The enemy tank armies broke through the border between First and Fourth Panzer Armies and surged deep into Galicia.

After three years learning it the hard way, the Red Army had now mastered German panzer tactics and developed them further while assembling masses of tanks and men. If the Russian tank tactics of 1941–2 had been unwieldy and disorganised, now they were the equal of the German *Blitzkrieg* in focus and manoeuvrability.

Here follows the calendar of Battalion 507 events for the period 4 July to 8 September containing the details of panzer actions and the diary entries of Eychmüller, Aichinger, Seefried, Raab, Gutmann and Obermayr. Then come, approximately chronologically, the experiences of Beck, Hagenberger, Diez, Durst, Eychmüller, Kramer and Zinke.

Calendar and Diary Entries

30 June 1944

OBERMAYR: Rail transport from Zloczov. Waited at Lublin.

1 July 1944

OBERMAYR: Crossed the Bug at Chermeka (40 km from Grabarka) and then via Yasinovka and Narewka.

2 July 194

OBERMAYR: At 0900 train passed through Slonim. Towards midday we arrived at Baranovicze and were unloaded at 1800 hrs. Then we drove to the assembly point.

A Soviet SU-152 self-propelled gun waiting at a readiness position, summer 1944.

3 July 1944

AICHINGER: Unloaded at Baranovicze and drove 12 km to battalion assembly point.

OBERMAYR: 0100 hrs left with 1st Company. Went to a position on a height.

SEEFRIED: Our SPW (driver Martin Braun) threw a track. I got out to help him. We came across some wounded to whom I gave first aid. Then we were attacked directly by a bomber. A signal rocket followed the bombs. We took cover in a field, pressed to the earth. Once the attack finished we had no casualties and could continue work on the track. When we arrived at Singaska it was past midnight.

4 July 1944

AICHINGER: In a wood near Litva we came under attack by US-built aircraft. 1st Company was deployed against an enemy attack from the south-east.

EYCHMÜLLER/DIEZ: Counter-attack against Kleck.

OBERMAYR: New formation. Attack on Kleck against Hungarians who had changed sides.

SEEFRIED: At 0800 hrs we advanced with orders to free the Hungarian prisoners at Kleck. On the way, Walter's SPW got stuck in a ditch and could not get free. The house nearby began to burn. Since the heat could set off the ammunition and explosive charges, we jettisoned them. Later two SPWs towed us out and then we took part in the fierce house-to-house fighting for Kleck. It made a dreadful picture, everywhere dead or wounded Hungarians. The resistance in Kleck itself was soon broken; after that we languished in the blazing sun on watch. In the evening we pulled out: the Hungarians we had freed went with us. When we got back to Singaska, everything was being blown up.[1]

5 July 1944

EYCHMÜLLER: Attack on Yatviez.

OBERMAYR: In the early morning we were near Baranovicze again.

AICHINGER: From Muskievicze we experienced an air raid on Baranovicze and the approach road. The main battle line is being pulled back 20 km.

---

1. To judge by the statements of Obermayr and Seefried, there would appear to have been a mutiny at Kleck in which pro-Soviet Hungarian elements seized control of the town, imprisoned the pro-German Hungarian loyalists and then took on the Germans.

Two Tigers of 507 Battalion on rail low-loaders. The one on the left has the old running wheels (one pair is missing) and is fitted with the broad operational tracks. Tiger 323 has the narrow transport tracks suggesting that it is returning to Germany. Its broad tracks would be stowed on the Ssyms-wagon below the panzer.

This photo shows clearly how the narrow tracks fitted within the outer gear rims, and that the outer running wheels have been removed. This was necessary because on the German rail network the electricity pylons stood too close to the permanent way and might be struck by the broad field tracks.

A Tiger of 1st Company, 507th Battalion, waiting for a second recovery vehicle on a woodland track. Behind the panzer is an 18-tonne Famo tractor which was not capable of towing a Tiger alone.

German troops have been surrounded at Minsk. Six men were wounded by the bombing.

SEEFRIED: We came to a village where it was quiet all day. In the afternoon we entered a neighbouring village where all cattle were slaughtered in expectation of our being encircled. When we returned to 'our' village it had just

In this photo taken by a Propaganda Company correspondent, Tiger 113
is seen passing through a burning village. The number has not been
painted on the spare track segments.

Tiger 100 (1st Company command panzer) has its number painted on the
track segments. This was a feature on many 507 Battalion Tigers.

been ravaged by aircraft and half of it was in flames. We stood security again
at night.

6 July 1944
EYCHMÜLLER: Attacked Viedzma and advanced south of Zalubicze.

A side view of 507 Staff Company Tiger C.. The running wheels show that this panzer still has the old chassis. A feature of all Staff Tigers was a star aerial at the rear for radio communication with higher levels.

AICHINGER: We are at Czepielov.

OBERMAYR: 0200 hrs as radio post for 3rd Company. Heavy artillery and Pak fire!

SEEFRIED: In the early morning we roasted some poultry. At 1300 hrs orders came to take provisions to 3rd Company east of us. On the way we were met by its Tigers heading towards us and even the infantry were pulling back. There was talk that we were encircled. Back at 'our' village, Ivan was bombarding it with Stalin organs so that everything seemed to be on fire. We left the place as quickly as we could and sheltered in a nearby wood until nightfall. At about 2200 hrs when the retreat continued we were the tail SPW and so when we shed both tracks our disquiet can be imagined. We set to work until suddenly hearing shouting in the darkness which seemed to be in Russian. A sergeant and I went cautiously nearer, machine pistols and hand grenades at the ready. As some figures passed by we scarcely dared breathe, we were that close to them but they failed to notice us. Finally the driver Walther came to report that the tracks had been refitted and soon we roared off in pursuit of the other SPWs.

7 July 1944

EYCHMÜLLER: Security duty on the main battle line. We counter-attacked south-east of Baranovicze to clean up.

OBERMAYR: Back to Baranovicze. Broken down in A Platoon: Braun and Lindenbauer.

SEEFRIED: After driving all night we received the radioed order 'SPW platoon proceed spearhead direction sun.' As we set off eastwards some Russians ahead took to their heels. Suddenly the fuel canister on Braun's SPW was on fire, and we saw Martin hang it over the side and then toss it away. He got back aboard, and a second later received a direct hit from an enemy tank which had suddenly appeared.

Bobby and I jumped out and ran to Braun's SPW to find a horrific scene of carnage: on the driving seat only half of Lindenbauer was recognisable, and Braun lay stretched out in the vehicle, also dead; only Stelzig was still alive, but with a serious leg wound. I took him on my shoulder and carried him through the enemy fire to the nearest SPW. Upon returning to my own vehicle I found Dutzler and Bindl also seriously wounded. As we drove back we bogged down in a swamp. To add to our woes, a T-34 appeared on our flank: we feared the worst until driver Steidl came up and towed us free at the last moment. Braun's SPW was beyond repair and in the evening a Tiger shot it in flames. On the withdrawal which followed we passed through the burning Baranovicze. The Russians were closing in.

8 July 1944

EYCHMÜLLER: Engaged in fighting at Piotrovicze and Polonka.

AICHINGER: After a drive of 75 km we reached Volkovysk. We were hit by a Pak and had six dead and several wounded. We lost two Tigers and an SPW.

OBERMAYR: Assembly area near Baranovicze. V Company gave cover against partisans in the woods. A Platoon had more losses. Arrival at Slonim.

SEEFRIED: We were at Hinczevicze when everybody received the order at 0800 hrs: 'Panzer Battalion 507 will advance today to break out of the encirclement.' We were to go with V Company to the *Rollbahn*. As soon as we started we were attacked by *Jabos* [fighter-bombers]. I got a splinter in the back. Suddenly a lorry was hit and its cargo of ammunition went up. One of the Panzer IVs ahead was hit and burned. Unteroffizier Sauer, too, moving up with his SPW, received a hit from a 9.2 cm Pak of US manufacture. When I went forward with Bobby to help, we brought out Schilldorfer of the

Reconnaissance Company, but all the rest were dead. A terrible sight! Bobby jumped into the SPW, started it up, reversed a bit under my directions but the track was torn on one side so that the wagon side-slipped and stopped. Feldwebel Rühe towed us off to the repair yard where we buried our dead. After that I went to the main dressing station.

9 July 144

EYCHMÜLLER: Defensive actions to the east and in the northern part of Slonim.

OBERMAYR: At Slonim we buried Unteroffizier Sauer and Gefreiters Sauer, Netroval and Busch.

10 July 1944

OBERMAYR: Went to repair yard at Zielenika. A Tiger crushed the VW Kübelwagen of Unteroffizier Knoche while reversing.

SEEFRIED: All our SPWs are with the repairs staff. In the early hours while cleaning weapons Höfinger shot himself in the thigh with his pistol. Towards 1400 hrs we drove back.

11 July 1944

OBERMAYR: Drove back to Volkovysk on a fine asphalt road.

SEEFRIED: For the next fourteen days we stayed with the Workshop Company.

12 July 1944

EYCHMÜLLER: Defensive operations in Zelvianka sector.

13 July 1944

EYCHMÜLLER: Defensive operations at Miedzyrzecz in the Klepacze sector.

OBERMAYR: Leutnant Sederl and Goliasch wounded.

14 July 1944

OBERMAYR: Assembly area, in woods as radio post.

15 July 1944

EYCHMÜLLER: Attack at Zanki.

OBERMAYR: Drove with Major Schmidt to battalion command post. In the evening moved back westwards.

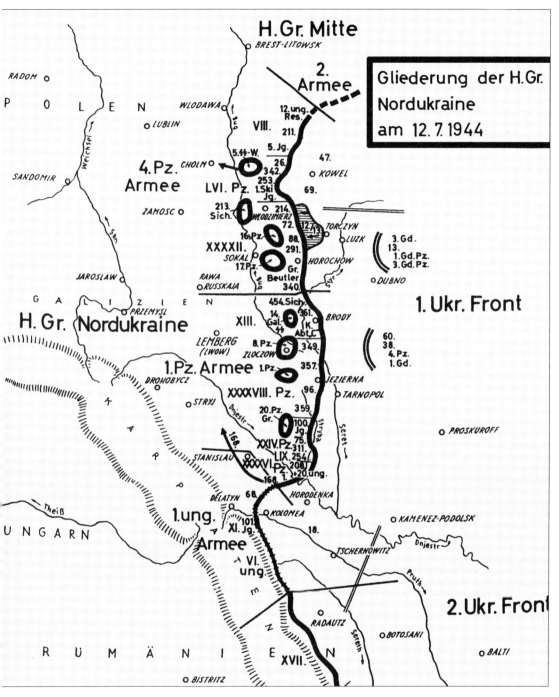

Map extract showing the organisation of Army Group North Ukraine on 12 July 1944. Brody, recaptured in the spring, was still in the battle area at this point while Tarnopol had been lost. The collapse of Army Group Centre in the summer of 1944 led to dramatic changes in all sectors of the front.

16 July 1944

EYCHMÜLLER: Attack, withdrawal at Kryki.

17 July 1944

EYCHMÜLLER: North-east of Chrustov.

19 July 1944

EYCHMÜLLER: Secured the front east of Potoziermi and rearguard action east of Novy Vola.

20 July 1944

EYCHMÜLLER: Secured bridge and counter-attack at Trzeszczotki.

OBERMAYR: Attempt on Führer's life. A general arrived by Fieseler Storch.

A tough-looking group of panzer-grenadiers waiting by a Tiger for the next attack.

21 July 1944

EYCHMÜLLER: Counter-attacking south of Trzeszczotki.

OBERMAYR: Attacking 1 km north-east of Odryniki.

22 July 1944

EYCHMÜLLER: Counter-attacking south of Trzeszczotki.

OBERMAYR: 0300 hrs back over the Nev.

23 July 1944

EYCHMÜLLER: Secured Loknica sector.

RAAB: Counter-attacked south of Ogrodniki.

24 July 144

EYCHMÜLLER: Counter-attacked in Loknica sector.

25 July 1944

OBERMAYR: Feldwebel Rühl took over A Platoon (Staff Company).

26 July 1944

RAAB: Attack on Koscele-Scernie.

SIEGFRIED: Left the workshops and reached battalion in a wood near Bielsk. In the night the withdrawal continued.

27 July 1944

RAAB: Attack on Tubiazyn.

EYCHMÜLLER: Fought during withdrawal at Saki and Zubovo.

SEEFRIED: During the day it fell quiet. Towards 0930 hrs we went to Kollonya as radio relay post.

OBERMAYR: Drove southwards towards Bielsk. Attacked with 3rd Company.

AICHINGER: At Vlosty Olszanka we dug in our staff car against splinter damage.

28 July 1944

EYCHMÜLLER: Counter-attacked at Biala.

RAAB: Attacked at Krasna-Vies.

A Tiger of 2nd Company, 3rd Platoon, pausing for a break in a village.

SEEFRIED: Remained at Kollonya until evening when relieved by Steidl.

29 July 1944

RAAB: Attacked eastwards near Bielsk

EYCHMÜLLER: Attacked Dubiazyn and Bosianovka.

SEEFRIED: Instruction and weapons cleaning. At 1800 hrs we proceeded to Banky as radio post, then at 2100 hrs were ordered to pull out immediately: we received fresh instructions from our command post.

30 July 1944

RAAB: Attacked Augustov.

GUTMANN: Attacked Raysk and Pulsze.

SEEFRIED: We waited in a wood all day. At 1800 hrs we were bringing up rations for the companies. As we came to open country beyond the wood heavy artillery fire forced us to return. We took with us three wounded: Leutnant Pfeuffer, a *Feldwebel* and a loader. Then we took over the radio post at Strichy. Shortly after midnight we received the order to pull back. At Malesche we set three houses on fire and butchered the cattle. A civilian who refused to obey our order to leave the village was also shot dead.

31 July1944

SEEFRIED: At 0400 hrs we reached the battalion command post, in the evening the withdrawal continued.

1 August 1944

AICHINGER: Waited north of Zambrov, 6 km from the *Rollbahn*.

GUTMANN: On Height 169 eastwards of Hodyszev.

RAAB: Counter-attacked north of Mien.

SEEFRIED: At 0500 hrs we went forward as radio post but returned at 0700 hrs. Over the next few days nothing of importance occurred.

2 August 1944

GUTMANN: Mopped up breakthrough south of Liza Stara.

EYCHMÜLLER: Wilkov.

3 August 1944

GUTMANN: Defending line south-east Sciony.

EYCHMÜLLER: Height 140.7, west of Lunaz.

AICHINGER: Crossed the Narew and set up a base. In a handbill General-feldmarschall Model exhorted us to advance against the enemy.

4 August 1944

GUTMANN: Fighting to secure the line south-east of Scinoy.

SEEFRIED: 1300 hrs: Bobby received the Iron Cross Second Class.

5 August 1944

SEEFRIED: We played football.

6 August 194

SEEFRIED: At 1015 hrs an alert. We drove to brigade.

Tiger B here is still fitted with the old running wheels and rubber tyres.
The panzer has a rod aerial on the turret and a star aerial at the rear.
A spare star aerial can be seen stowed at the stern.

RAAB: Attacked Height 158.1, east of Lupianka.

EYCHMÜLLER: Zanilov. On Height 140.7.

7 August 1944
RAAB: Attacked east of Lupianka.

SEEFRIED: The village ahead of us was under attack all day from Russian *Jabos*. One machine crashed in flames, the pilot baled out and was captured. He is a highly decorated sergeant. Bobby brought along a small dog and in the afternoon we gave him a good bath.

8 August 1944
GUTMANN: North-east Hodyszev.

SEEFRIED: We held the Russians until evening, then withdrew farther west via Sokoly.

9 August 1944

SEEFRIED: In our crew there are misunderstandings. I had to see Feldwebel Rühl to discuss the matter.

10 August 1944

SEEFRIED: Schmelzer and Bobby are being replaced by Utzig and Hausmann.

11 August 1944

SEEFRIED: We drove to the repairs staff via Lomsha then looked for an inn.

14 August 1944

SEEFRIED: When our vehicle was serviceable again we went via Ostrov to battalion.

15 August 1944

AICHINGER: Oberschirrmeister [Motor-pool Superintendent] Deutschmann left for officer training in the Reich. Mühl is replacing him.

SEEFRIED: I have received the Wound Badge. Towards midnight we drove to an assembly area.

A Propaganda Company photo of Staff Tiger B, late summer 1944. Nearly all Tiger Is had the leading outer running wheel missing although the Tiger I was delivered from the factory with four.

16 August 1944

SEEFRIED: At 0400 hrs we moved out for another attack. We had contact with the enemy at 0600 hrs. The Russian artillery was very active. Suddenly *Jabos* appeared and attacked at once. Now began a very unpleasant concert. At 1000 hrs we drove to brigade with Major Schmidt and then to 5th Regiment where we received orders to take an artillery spotter ahead of our lines. As we did that at 1530 hrs we received fire from a Pak. We crossed the field this way and that in the attempt to get out of range before finally reaching a wood where the *Jabos* found us. We jumped back into the SPW but they were remorseless with their bombs, rockets and guns. Under the numerous near misses the vehicle shook from side to side. Luck was on our side and we escaped the inferno. Towards 1800 hrs we retired to the wood near Kolaki.

17 August 1944

OPERATIONAL ORDERS: '1st and 2nd Companies: *Rollbahn* Zambrov–Bialystok.'

SEEFRIED: At 0500 mounted new attack, broken off at 0800 hrs. We drove back to Kolaki, and in the evening arrived at Soltys as radio post.

18 August 1944

SEEFRIED: At Soltys until evening when we were stood down and drove to Viyotta to direct traffic from 2200 hrs until 0400 hrs next morning.

19 August 1944

SEEFRIED: We followed behind the battalion and rejoined it in a wood where at 1500 hrs Major Schmidt took his leave of us. Hauptmann Fritz Schöck has taken over as commanding officer of the battalion.

20 August 1944

SEEFRIED: Nothing special to report.

OBERMAYR: Schöck is taking over the battalion.

21 August 1944

SEEFRIED: At midnight, an alarm! The enemy has broken through at Zambrov. We had to direct traffic into the readiness area. We came in for so much attention from night bombers that we spent more time lying on the ground than standing.

A delivery of Tigers for 507 Battalion at Sanok railway station. These were deployed with Army Group South in 1944.

22 August 1944

OPERATIONAL ORDERS: '1st, 2nd and 3rd Companies: Counter-attacks and defend north-west of Zambrov.'

SEEFRIED: At 0700 hrs Ivan began an artillery barrage with Stalin Organ accompaniment. We could not move out with our SPW. Ten Tigers bogged down in the swamp and had to be destroyed. We held out until 0900 hrs then were forced to withdraw. The situation is beyond our control. As we pulled out we were attacked on the *Rollbahn* by *Jabos*. They dropped their bombs directly on the highway. Martin Bauer received a head wound. Our panzers have heavy losses. Leutnant Lischka fell. By evening we had shaken off the enemy.

23 August 1944

OPERATIONAL ORDERS: '1st and 3rd Companies: Defend around Czervony-Bor.'

SEEFRIED: During the day there was a lull. At 1830 hrs we advanced carrying infantry as passengers to their positions. At 1900 hrs our attack began. By then it was fairly dark. We were in hilly bushland covering the rear and flanks. It was a very nervy time. Nearby some Russian MGs began to chatter. The situation was damned critical. At 2300 hrs we pulled out and arrived at a wood at 0400 hrs. We slept nearly all the next day.

24 August 1944

OPERATIONAL ORDERS: '1st and 3rd Companies: defend north-west of Sniadov.'

OBERMAYR: The commander of 3rd Company has been promoted to *Hauptmann*.

25 August 1944

OPERATIONAL ORDERS: '1st and 3rd Companies: defend north-west of Sniadov.'

AICHINGER: Yednorocze. Fuel transports. Two killed by aircraft.

SEEFRIED: We indicated the route for the companies by putting up shields. Driving back, a panzer handed us the body of Leutnant Lautmann who had been killed in the air raid. We took his body into the woods and buried him there. At night we guided the Supply Company into a wood east of Debov and returned to the command post at 0500 hrs. Otherwise nothing to report.

27 August 1944

OPERATIONAL ORDERS: '3rd Company, counter-attack from Chrostov to the south. 2nd Company, south-east of Debov.'

SEEFRIED: We accompanied 3rd Company as radio post.

28 August 1944

SEEFRIED: Ivan launched an attack, this was crushed by our Tigers.

29 August 1944

OPERATIONAL ORDERS: '1st Company, Piski.'

SEEFRIED: The enemy resumed blasting at us at 0500 hrs, boxing us in with artillery and *Jabos* with the aim of recapturing Grossdov Ladimansk. In the evening we returned to the readiness position.

30 August 1944

SEEFRIED: We have been mentioned in the *Wehrmacht Bulletin*: 'Heavy Panzer Battalion 507, led by Knight's Cross holder Major Schmidt, distinguished itself especially by outstanding steadfastness and cleverly executed counter-attacks.' At 1600 hrs we drove to the Narew to reconnoitre a fording point for the Tigers. We took the opportunity to have a refreshing bathe.

31 August 1944

OBERMAYR: The corps command post has transferred to the other side of the Narew.

SEEFRIED: We drove to Ladicin as radio post.

1 September 1944

SEEFRIED: Fifth anniversary of the outbreak of the war. Nothing else to report.

2 September 1944

SEEFRIED: We went to the battalion command post in a wood south of Govorka.

3 September 1944

OPERATIONAL ORDERS: '1st Company, Troszyn. 2nd Company, fighting north-east Dabeck.'

SEEFRIED: I was awoken by an air raid. Today Ivan attempted unsuccessfully to capture Scharfenwiese.

4 September 1944

SEEFRIED: Air attacks all day without pause. Towards evening some Pak rounds went so wide that they wrecked the field telephone hanging at the back of the SPW.

6 September 1944

OPERATIONAL ORDERS: '1st and 2nd Companies: secure south-west Napiorki.'

SEEFRIED: The morning passed quietly. At 1600 hrs we delivered rations forward and then I directed traffic until next morning.

7 September 1944

SEEFRIED: At 0830 hrs Russian artillery bombarded our wood. I sought cover in Oberleutnant Wirsching's Tiger. We left the wood at 1400 hrs. At 1700 hrs Hauptmann Schöck was summoned by a colonel (name unknown) to receive from his hand the award of the Knight's Cross.

8 September 1944

SEEFRIED: We lay under Russian artillery fire all day.

9 September 1944

SEEFRIED: I think I have caught something dreadful. Spent all day in bed in the tent. I felt so bad that I didn't get up even for artillery near misses. A towing tractor brought me back to base, then I rested in an ambulance.

11 September 1944

SEEFRIED: Apparently it is dysentery and at 1300 hrs I was taken to the main dressing station at Mackeim. I lay there in a ruined house until about 2100 hrs before being brought to the military hospital at Praschnitz and admitted there until 25 September.

12 September 1944

AICHINGER: The battalion is moving towards Zichenau. Oberleutnant Peter Heesch is now commander of the Staff Company, Oberleutnant Schaup is in charge of the rear echelon, Oberfeldwebel Wolfram becomes the *Spiess* and Unteroffizier Klumpp near me the IA-clerk of Staff Company.

13 September 1944

OBERMAYR: At night we moved off to the woods at Rebkov.

Heinz Zinke (gunner, final rank *Unteroffizier*): The Undulating Road to Polonka

I had been discharged from the military hospital at Paderborn after recovering from my wound and now hoped to return to my old unit. I went with a Panzer Reserve Battalion 500 transport. Getting back to 'the mob' was not so easy at that time. The reserve battalions were fairly high-handed about who went where and one could even end up in a different branch of service!

Outer compound of the panzer repair works (south) at Sanok situated on the River San and at the foot of the Beskid mountains. Tigers, Hummel self-propelled guns, assault guns and other Wehrmacht vehicles can be seen in this photo.

Sanok, early summer 1944. Tigers from various battalions await repair.

Podhorce was where Battalion 507 had rested for a while after its first deployment in the Tarnopol–Brody area. Therefore I was very fortunate to get to Podhorce for a 'mustering out'. We paraded and Oberleutnant Neumeyer in company with *Spiess* Bäumler drove down the ranks in the Kübelwagen. I was the only man whom Bäumler recognised, and he had Neumeyer stop and ask if I could shoot. So I was 'employed' by him as a gunner.

At this time the Byelorussian Front had advanced, broken through our lines at Vitebsk and was now advancing smartly via Minsk. Since the Germans were retreating at the same rate, not least because some of our 'brothers-in-arms' were proving not to have the expected 'steadfastness', it was therefore understandable that Panzer Battalion 507 should be ordered to the centre of Army Group Centre as 'the fire brigade'.

The wonderful days at Podhorce were over. At the end of June the battalion was sent northwards by train and set down at Baranovicze. It went into action so to speak 'straight from the unloading ramp'. I do not remember the exact route but we were on the move the whole night and got to the assembly area at Baranovicze towards daybreak. After the necessary technical preparations we set out the same morning for the town of Polonka, 40 km away, where an enemy base had been identified.

The squadron set off through a sparse pine forest in which a kind of *Rollbahn* had developed. The terrain fell slightly downhill, the dry sandy ground causing a long banner of dust to fan out behind our file of Tigers. The wood ended after a few kilometres and the countryside ahead of us was barren of trees. The road rose and fell providing a wavelike impression and so we called it 'Waves of the Danube'. Our route passed from one crest of the undulating road to another until finally we arrived at the last hilltop before Polonka. Here we had a significant overview of the region. What was going on in Polonka itself could not be seen, for it stood hidden behind houses, trees and bushes.

It was about 2,000 m from our squadron of Tigers to the edge of town. After leaving the pine wood we had formed into a broad wedge in order to guard against surprises. Now we were in line on the reverse slope, looking down from the crest. There seemed to be no shortage of soldiers in town, of various branches of service, predominantly horse-drawn. After making the corresponding preparations we opened fire. The Soviets had apparently felt themselves fairly safe, for when our first salvoes arrived there was total chaos, people running around wildly, vehicles being driven in all directions at once.

The surprise effect did not last long, and very soon we received an accurate reply from heavy-calibre guns. This caused us our first unserviceable Tigers, mainly with damaged tracks. The shells, which came towards us from good cover, were well spread apart, leading us to conclude that we were under tank fire. Their camouflage was first-class and they could hardly be made out. First we had to use intact Tigers to tow back damaged Tigers from the crest to the dead ground, and after four hours of all this our unserviceable Tigers were so numerous that a general retreat was ordered.

Six serviceable Tigers were withdrawn from the crest to cover the withdrawal. After a while an enemy tank unit sortied out to exchange fire; they wore us down gradually until only two 3rd Company Tigers were left to cover the withdrawal over the undulating road. Since this towing business was not possible at top speed, the Russians were soon hot on our heels.

The two Tigers forming the rearguard had their guns pointing to six o'clock and held the enemy tanks at bay from each crest to give the squadron cover for as long as possible. At the last crest before the entrance to the pine wood we watched as twenty-five to thirty enemy tanks formed up into a broad wedge between 1,000 and 1,500 m away as if on exercise! Besides the known types we were very interested in some very large examples with a flat, semicircular turret and huge gun.

I aimed at these unknown types to disturb their advance – in vain! Previously with our 8.8 cm gun at this range we had never had difficulty in doing serious damage, but this time the hits ricocheted off. Finally the other rearguard Tiger reported a breakdown while I was now out of ammunition. As we went into the sparse woodland with our turret at six o'clock I could still see the enemy tank vanguard heading for us.

We moved close alongside our companion Tiger to ship aboard their last shells. Neumeyer suddenly made an emphatic demand for smoke. Fortunately in this regard I had obtained a good supply and soon we were enveloped in clouds of orange-red. Just at the right time too, for now several Stukas appeared overhead, probably a *Staffel*, and were soon howling and hurtling down towards the enemy spearhead with apparent success, for soon we saw their bombs exploding. The Stukas had saved us. Our joy was indescribable! As we heard later they were led by Ulrich Rudel.

Siegfried Beck: A Prisoner in the Warsaw Uprising

On operations after the unloading at Baranovicze, our Tiger 311 of which I was the driver dropped out with damaged gears. At the same time I reported sick, was diagnosed with lead poisoning and transferred to the military hospital at Warsaw. I had more or less recovered and had my written orders in my pocket to return to my unit when on 1 August 1944 at 1630 hrs the

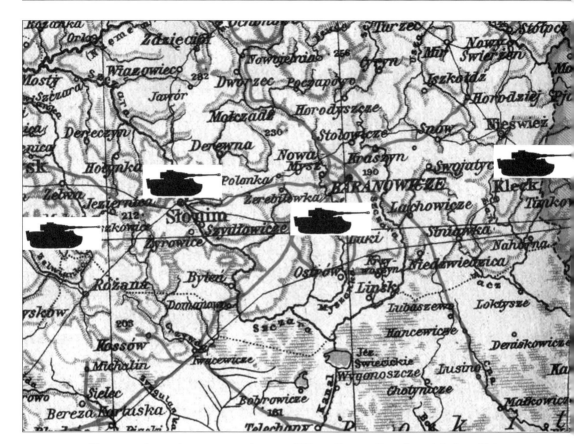

This map shows the operational areas of Heavy Panzer Battalion 507 from Zelwa
through Slonim and Baranovicze to Kleck in 1944.

'Warsaw Uprising' began. It was chaotic because the Poles were wearing
German uniforms.

I got through to the Vistula bridge and came across a platoon of SS-
Regiment *Germania* equipped with Tigers. They were short of a driver and
so to the general amusement of all I was made an SS-man by donning the
Germania cuff-title and took over the role for which I had been trained in
their panzer.

On the seventh day at the Marschalltovska crossroads near the main railway
station the panzer received a direct hit. I was the only crew member to get
out, but was then hit by infantry fire and collapsed. I regained consciousness
to find myself surrounded by insurgents. A lady who was about to slit my
throat was prevented from doing so by the others. There then followed two
dreadful months of beatings while living in constant fear that I would be
killed in a German raid or by the Poles. The insurgents had my Hitler Youth
Leaders' identity card and would always greet me with 'Now Hitler Youth,

later Gestapo' before handing out the next beating. Only later did it become clear that their boundless hatred for me was the result of the indefensible circumstances in force in the Warsaw ghetto since 1940 and from the incredibly brutal procedures of the SS (Special Unit *Dirlewanger*) in putting down the uprising.

On the other hand a Polish officer calling himself General Baronovorski had me tell him something about Tiger tanks. Two days before the insurgents capitulated I was freed by German commandos and spent the remainder of the war in a military hospital at Bad Tölz.

Richard Durst: Memories of Feldwebel Eberl

In the weeks after the rail transport and the unloading at Baranovicze we were always moving back westwards, accompanied continually by the deadly music of the Stalin Organ. On one of these first operational days at the heart of Army Group Centre a pig's carcass had been hung up for butchering in the 3rd Company field kitchen. A salvo from the Stalin Organ exploded in our midst, destroying the carcass. I was lightly wounded. Our Repairs Group Leader, Feldwebel Eberl, was so seriously wounded that he died on the way to the main field hospital at Baranovicze. Hermann Henne and I had to bury him there and then in the presence of an Army pastor who spoke a few words. In the staff car no. WH 1568386 in which Eberl was being transported there was also a badly burned *Oberfeldwebel*. He wore the Knight's Cross and was a member of a 'tank-cracker unit'. I have often wondered if he survived.

Gerd Eychmüller:
Operations in the Central Sector of the Eastern Front

After the unloading I was a platoon commander in 1st Company from Zloczov to Baranovicze. The entries in my *Soldbuch* relating to days engaged in operations run from 4 July to 6 September 1944, and geographically from Kleck to Napioli. In the following account I remember situations which I cannot arrange in strict chronological order and so I mention first a day which was much the same as the others (except for the greeting by the division CO).

1st Company had quarters in a village. Except for the sentries, the crews slept. In the earliest hour they were awoken abruptly by the thunder of an artillery barrage. Ivan was therefore about to launch an attack on the positions in front of us. I had a slightly uncomfortable feeling in the stomach region and heard at the same time, 'Company commanders to Commanding Officer!' and soon after that, 'Platoon leaders to Company Commander!'

There my colleagues and I were each given the *extract* of a map (in itself a rare occurrence) on which the routes to our operational areas were marked. After brief instructions to our panzer commanders we set off with the task of supporting our infantry in the field in their defence of the expected onslaught. I therefore remember this particular day because I had orders to report my platoon to the main command post of an infantry division. There an ecstatic welcome awaited us in which the division CO, a friendly, well-loved general, almost embraced the platoon's four 8.8 cm guns in his joyful relief since they would greatly strengthen the firepower of his men.

He dismissed us to proceed to the forward lines but not until his 'paymaster' (probably a staff quartermaster or similar) had fetched a bottle of schnapps for each panzer crew, which we received with thanks and stowed carefully against breakage for use after the mission concluded. We Tiger men were very impressed by the welcome we got from the infantry, their waving and rejoicing as they emerged from their trenches making us aware once more of the high regard in which we were held as a 'privileged clique'.

Things which occurred frequently in the retreats were bogging down in swampy land and having a track ride up over the drive wheel or come off against the undercarriage. This was generally cured by taking off the track and inserting new segments. I remember one case in particular in which all efforts proved in vain. Our Tiger had shed its tracks and bogged down in a swamp on the wheels. The Russian infantry, which we had raked with MG fire beforehand, were now closing in, and after quickly dismantling the radio equipment, the five of us 'homeless' panzer men sought refuge in another Tiger of my platoon which now had ten men inside it instead of five. By radio I ordered no shooting until I gave the order. The first of their infantry had crept up warily to the abandoned Tiger, went round it, then climbed up the hull, some of them disappearing inside. Now I gave the order to open fire and destroy the panzer. Whether any of the Russians survived I never found out. It did nothing to assuage my contrition at losing my panzer.

In a letter to my parents of 27 August 1944 (according to my *Soldbuch* on the 25th of the month I was north-west of Sniadov), I wrote these lines:

'My guardian angel has spread his wings once more above me. The day before yesterday I was forced to abandon again after a battle with enemy tanks.

Opposite & next page: A series of photos taken by Sebastian Hüpfl, then with Tiger 221. (By the end of the war he was an *Unteroffizier* and the gunner in Tiger 201.)
Above right: Three of his crew-mates by their tank.
Right: A solid earth bunker with a sign for the crew of Tiger 221.

Hüpfl's photos were probably taken in the summer of 1944.

An *Unteroffizier*, presumably the commander of Tiger 221, at the entrance
to their bunker.

All the crew got out except the driver who had an awful end. Although this happened very close to the Russian lines, we got back to our unit more or less unscathed. Early yesterday I drove back to the baggage train to fetch the most essential items of clothing because naturally I lost everything again. Yesterday afternoon I drove with my old company commander [Oberleutnant Neumeyer] into a small German frontier town [Scharfenwiese?]. We watched a German film, had a glass of beer and after all that lay behind us felt almost at home. It was a quite special experience to see small, clean German houses again and to hear German being spoken (not only by soldiers). This afternoon I am going forward to take over a new panzer already allotted to me. For the moment it is fairly do or die but we shall come through it – gritting my teeth until it's over. Now I must close, I have to drive to the workshop to look the panzer over. Heartfelt wishes, Your Gerd.'

To conclude my 'Spotlight' on engagements in Army Group Centre's sector (according to my *Soldbuch* there were twenty-four) I would like to mention a rather amusing incident. In the fighting during the retreat, as is known, our battalion was subordinated for a while to I Cavalry Corps (Harteneck). During this time I was engaged one day in building a defensive line forward of a row of hills. Before it the bald terrain fell slightly towards a large, dense forest about 2000 m distant, occupied by the Russians, and from inside it one could hear clearly the sounds of tracked vehicles. Suddenly a small Kübelwagen drew up and a lieutenant alighted, announcing himself as the aide-de-camp of a unit attached to the Cavalry Corps and passed me the following order from his commanding officer: 'In the wood in front of you are Russian tanks; drive your panzers into that wood and destroy them!' I replied that I required the order in writing. The lieutenant looked at me nonplussed and I explained: 'Not so that I will do it, but because according to my instructions I have to report the order to channels and through them to the General-Inspector of Panzer Troops, General Guderian.' The lieutenant gave me a slightly quizzical look then saluted, got back into his car and was never seen again.

Hubert Hagenberger: From Polonka to Slonim

We came down the transporter ramp at Baranovicze and headed for the radio masts I mentioned. The log road was very narrow in places so that many drivers slipped off it. We came through safely, which had a very favourable outcome a few days later.

It was fairly hot and radio silence was in force. Everybody was keyed up with fearful expectations of what lay before us. We were soon forced to leave the *Rollbahn* because it was totally blocked by army vehicles which had been abandoned during the withdrawal. What a discouraging sight! Thousands of vehicles, amongst them new SP assault guns, crewless. Between them were some burning lorries. Their drivers had simply legged it in panic.

'Prepare for action,' our fatherly panzer commander Bruno Bethge ordered. I closed my hatch in subdued mood. After a few kilometres driving near the *Rollbahn* we came to an abandoned village. I remember its admirable cobbled pavements along the broad uphill street. We were the leading panzer and Bethge told me to halt for a man in railway uniform coming towards us waving his cap. There was a brief exchange which I did not hear. I had the impression that he came from the railway junction at Sluzk to where we were bound.

Whatever the reason we continued to a wood on our left hand from which up to a dozen German infantrymen emerged, led by a general, face covered in dust, an MP 40 at the ready. I wondered if this was our main front line, for the general was indicating that a wood a few kilometres farther on was where the Russians were.

On the road leading to this wood was a depression where some houses with straw roofs formed a small village. The convoy of panzers came to a halt and in the headphones we heard Neumeyer's voice say, 'To everybody, wedge formation.'

We veered to the right and at once our Tiger sank down to the undercarriage in a watery meadow. I could not reverse us free but some logs from the road laid behind the tracks enabled the panzer to reverse out and reach terra firma.

Next we followed a road to arrive at the *Rollbahn* which went from Bobruisk via Sluzk westwards (three years before we Germans had marked it out in the opposite direction). The village ahead was said to be held by the Russians and from intercepted radio traffic we assumed that enemy tanks were massing in the woods. As it happened we needed to take no further action and became spectators as a *Staffel* of Stukas arrived.

'Quick, put the flag out!' Bethge shouted. In a flash the Reich war flag was fixed across the stern of the panzer and our frontline was indicated to the Stukas by flares; shortly after with sirens howling they tipped over and fell towards the village and woods. We saw the flashes and fire as the bombs exploded and also a column of fire marking the probable crash site of a Ju 87. This Stuka unit was almost certainly led by the 'tank-cracker' Oberst Rudel. The rapid-fire cannons built into the gull wings were distinctly recognisable, and we watched their effect. One after another black columns of smoke rising above the wood confirmed that on this occasion our work had been done for us.

The show was not yet over for now came the cavalry. 'That's a Hungarian unit,' Bethge shouted as he watched them gallop past, enveloped in dust, leaning forward on their steeds as once Attila's warriors had done. The hordes of Genghis Khan must have looked like this! But these Hungarians were fleeing in panic, only horses and riders, without wagons or guns, wrapped in a gigantic cloud of dust, which still had not settled long after the spectacle had passed.

We got back on the *Rollbahn* and ran down to the village in the trough between two hills. Some of the surviving houses in which we suspected a Russian presence were burning, but there was no sign of life except from a hut where somebody waved, and raised himself gingerly from the ground.

'They're Hungarians!' Bethge shouted and gave orders to approach. A Hungarian officer reported the situation to him. We had misjudged the situation and done wrong by our 'allies'. The Russians were behind the woods from where columns of smoke still rose into the blue skies from their burning vehicles. As we dismounted from the Tiger, Franz Pass spotted a pig on the loose and gave chase. After catching the animal he tied it up with telephone cable from the reel in the undercarriage and secured it to the ribs of the radiator grille where it continued to squeal. This soon got on our nerves but was tolerable for the thought of roast pork and sausages to come. When food was to be found, Franz was unsurpassed. He was the organiser to whom everybody was indebted for the reserves in their backpacks, from flour to cognac.

As I approached one of the still intact houses, I heard a whimpering and groaning coming from below. The entrance to an earth bunker, covered by a square wooden lid, led down 3 m. '*Ida suda!*' I shouted down, at which an elderly and gaunt woman wearing a headscarf appeared and began climbing the wooden ladder. She probably had a shock at seeing the death's head badges on the collar patches of my field tunic, then fell at my feet and kissed my filthy shoes. I thought this was weird but didn't laugh. She pointed to what once had been a house and was now a heap of rubble. '*Malinki*,' she said and spread the fingers of her raised hand towards it. There had probably been five children in the house and now all were gone, the contents of the house and all happiness. I had no time to reflect, nor time for sympathy.

'*Wod jest?*' she stammered, and looking around me I noticed on the road a smoking Hungarian field kitchen.

'*Woda*,' I agreed and we went to it. She put a green bottle to her lips but spat it out immediately, it was probably vinegar or soup seasoning. When I lifted the lid of the cauldron I found the ingredients for the midday meal, beans and

Soviet assault troops advancing in the summer of 1944.

water. I handed her a full ladle of it. Once she had finished it she fell at my feet again, cried, 'Jesus Maria' then returned to her earth bunker, apparently strengthened. As a 20-year-old I felt strangely moved by this episode.

In a meadow near the village street was a Kübelwagen flying a pennant from which I concluded that it had once served a senior officer as his wheels – perhaps it had belonged to the infantry general we had met recently. The noise of battle had died away completely. We all returned to the panzer to take up a security position but the Russians did not come again that day which pleased us. At dusk, however, there appeared a shadowy form going 'put-put' above us, the 'Duty NCO'.

Hubert Hagenberger: Stabsfeldwebel Bethge's Last Day

Reports came flooding in by the dozen. Air reconnaissance showed that 320 enemy tanks were moving out from Polonka. Our Tigers had to stop them. Since leaving the railway ramp at Baranovicze on 2 July, we had seen our army in flight and disintegration. All must have been assailed by panic, the fires stoked by *Jabo* and partisan attacks.

The weather was hot. I sat next to the hot gearbox where I could find some relief by squatting on the backrest, a foot on the gas pedal, my head through the hatch for fresh air. In this way I would drive through waving fields of corn. Our panzers also suffered from the heat: some failed to reach the area of operations due to engines overheating.

Now we were pushing forward in a fan formation towards a rounded hilltop behind which we assumed the enemy was lurking. Personally I was not greatly keen to follow the course of battle through my viewing slit: I thought of Ludwig Gsandner who had had his nose torn off when a round from an anti-tank rifle hit his viewing slit. If we were in the thick of it I would push myself back as far as possible while still having my foot on the gas pedal and able to accelerate the traverse of the turret when needed.

Now it rotated! Hits thundered against the armour making the interior paintwork flake. Bethge maintained an iron calm exuding confidence and security. Round after round we fired, the ventilator sucking out the powder smoke from the ejected casings. The clouds of dust which I could see over there suggested the presence of many enemy tanks, amongst them the heavy Josef Stalins and T-34s, which were not to be messed with: their 12.2 cm and long 7.62 cm guns respectively made them both the equal of the Tiger.

'So, that was the fifth,' Bethge said, his last words in life. Then we were hit as if by lightning. A metallic splitting noise followed the deafening explosions. Daylight streamed into the interior. Bethge had collapsed and fallen back into the turret. I resumed my position and tried to restart the engine which I had turned off but it would not respond. Probably a problem with the carburettor, I thought. Everybody was desperate to bale out. In a panic I scrambled free and ran several hundred metres while shells howled and hissed around me until at last I reached the edge of the cornfield and threw myself down.

Pass called to me, 'Bertl, what's happening?' I replied by gesticulating that he should get clear. It then occurred to me that perhaps I should have turned on the electric fuel pump above the armature panel in order to restart the engine. Our Tiger stood on a slope of the rounded hill, solitary and abandoned except for Stabsfeldwebel Bethge alive or dead inside it. Quickly I took the decision to return to the panzer and at least make one last attempt to save the vehicle and ascertain the condition of its commander.

As if I had received the order from Bethge myself, I ran to Schreiber's damaged panzer. At my request he drove me as far forward as he could while still hugging the reverse of the slope for cover. Then I sprinted the last stretch to 313. Gasping for breath I reached the stern and took a brief rest between the two exhaust covers. Our panzer unit had been forced to yield to the enemy's numerical superiority and pulled back. The noise of battle had abated somewhat but access to the driver's hatch was very tricky. I ran bent double alongside the wheels, then had to jump up on the track cover and dive through the hatch. I caught my overalls on the hatch lever and hung like that, upper body forward. As a result of my effort to reach the button for the injection pump I managed to tear free of the restraint and, thank heavens, I was in!

To start up and select fourth gear was now easy. The panzer ran back down: I waited for the right moment then brought the head round to face west, selected up to eighth gear, and roared off. I drove through waving fields into the sun: on the horizon were some poplars and a village. Near the first grey house was something squarish and grey which I could not make out. Driving with my head out I was without radio contact to the unit. From the village came a sudden lightning flash and 313 was hit. To my right lay a depression with a patch of beech trees. I careered through them, stopped the panzer and clambered into the radio operator's seat. I switched the equipment to 'Send' and stuttered in my excitement: 'Vehicle 313 here. I am in front of a village which is firing at me. Where should I go?'

At once came Neumeyer's calm voice, 'Yes, you've gone over to Ivan. We can see you from here. Turn ninety and a half right and then drive straight ahead until you reach us. What's up with Bethge and the rest of the crew?' Feverishly I supplied a brief answer and slipped back into the driving seat. Having made the turn ordered I drove like crazy. I heard the Russians firing at me from the rear but kept my head outside knowing that the gun turret would protect me. At last I caught sight of our unit, then the command Tiger 300 and pulled up alongside it.

Neumeyer was startled when I tapped him on the shoulder. 'So you're here, Hagenberger,' he said, and pointed towards the west. 'That cloud of dust you see is Feldwebel Schreiber, he's going to the workshops at Bialystok, follow him!'

'*Jawohl!*' I had driven some distance through more cornfields when, passing by a beechwood, I noticed a group waving to me to come in. Schreiber and my crew were already there. As Franzl gave me a coffee I told him, 'Look after Bethge, he's still in the panzer!' He was still alive when they lifted him out. He had lost his hands, his head was spattered with blood yet he raised the stump of an arm as if in a last salute. Could we have done more for him, this big, brave Berliner? Could he have been saved? These questions plague me even today. If he had lived, however, it would have been as a blind man with no hands. He died in the ambulance on the way to Slonim. I still mourn him today, father Bruno Bethge, for whom we were his 'boys'.

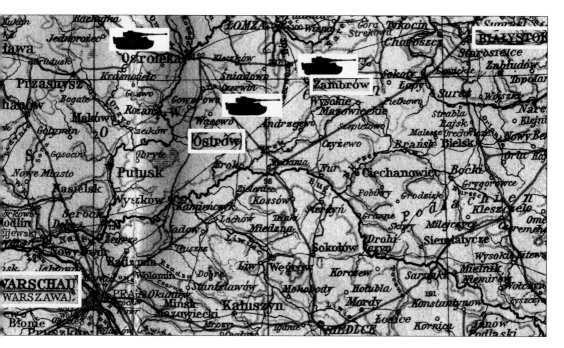

Battle area of Heavy Panzer Battalion 507 north-east of Warsaw,
late summer and autumn 1944.

Hubert Hagenberger: On the Road with Neumeyer

Schreiber was taking his Tiger to Slonim. It had received a hit on the cylindrical gun mantlet which meant that the weapon might require adjustment. We tailed along behind Schreiber since we had no commander. Everybody was in retreat, why not us? In the afternoon I was too exhausted to drive any more, partly as a result of partaking too much Serbian white wine a little earlier. Despite the noise I fell asleep under an oak near the *Rollbahn* and it was almost dark when we arrived at Slonim. On its streets an indescribable chaos reigned. People were fleeing. I saw a sudden flash from the pavement. A civilian had fired at Schreiber but missed. Two of us who had witnessed the incident jumped down from the panzer and seized him. I did not see what happened to him next. Without having realised it at first we were parked close by the army arsenal. When a drunken Pole came by clasping a bottle of red wine we enquired of him where he had got it and he pointed in the direction of a warehouse.

The crew of Tiger 305 of 3rd Company in the summer of 1944.
From left: Unteroffizier Kurt Kramer, radio operator; Leutnant Gerd Eychmüller, commander of 1st Platoon, a frequent guest; Oberleutnant Neumeyer, commander of 3rd Company; Unteroffizier Kurt Lehmann, driver; Unteroffizier Heinz Zinke, gunner; Gefreiter Gamsjäger, loader.

Heinz Zinke recalls the following episode at the Slonim Army Provisions Compound: 'I remember a young Wehrmacht administration official, who had not received orders to open up the warehouse, gesticulating in vain with his Walther pistol as a large number of German infantry forced in the gate. We too had a look round and then loaded some cartons and crates on the rear of our Tiger. On the continuing retreat whenever we overtook infantry and horse-drawn units we shared out 100-packs of 'Egypt' and 'Camel' cigarettes which were accepted with howls of joy!'

(Hagenberger continues.) Schreiber was no longer with us, leaving us practically 'leaderless' which would otherwise have inhibited us from entering the halls to help ourselves. Cigarettes lay in great mounds on the floor. We quickly became very selective and took only 'valuable wares': Egyptian cigarettes of the highest class, Schokakola drinks, flints, cut-throat razors and sides of bacon. Unfortunately there was no bread. The steering gear of 313 had failed and condemned us to a standstill. In this hopeless situation we shared out 100-packs of cigarettes to infantry hurrying by. On the pavement, people were slurping noisily from a barrel of beer. Somebody must have had a very impressive talk with a paymaster for all and sundry to have the run of the place like this.

The Russian artillery were already in range of the town, the odd round causing one or two houses to burn. Traffic was heading only westwards. Suddenly Placzek's panzer appeared in front of us. I told him my problem and he said at once, 'I'll give you a tow'. Once again he was my saviour! After his people had raided the warehouse for everything they needed and could carry we made off. By then the pace was hotting up and the air more dangerous with whizzing splinters.

The same group seated, at the right is a water container.

When we came to a wobbly wooden bridge over the broad Shachara River, a tributary of the Memel, field gendarmes redirected us to an island in the middle of the river. As we stood there, most of us in the open, without warning a concrete bridge nearby was demolished by a tremendous explosion. We ducked down near the wheels of our Tigers as great clumps of debris flew past overhead. Now we were free to turn about and drive back to the eastern bank. From there we headed to an intact road bridge farther up by which we crossed to the western bank. Here we were received by an infantry colonel who ordered us, 'Stay here with your guns facing east!'

We obeyed this order with reluctance but after some time were happy to observe a staff car containing high-ranking panzer officers including our battalion adjutant, Oberleutnant Koltermann, who ordered us to proceed towards Zelva. 'The last order is the holiest.'

On the way to Zelva we stopped for a rest in a field. In the afternoon, when retreating German infantry appeared over the hilltops coming towards us, we decided to resume heading westwards, but our misfortunes continued. Turning the panzer in the field resulted in so much earth clogging the running wheels that the track tightened and wouldn't move. It required seven hand grenades to get it off so that we could clear away the earth. Then it had to be refitted, replacing the damaged segments and bolts. It was dusk when we were finally roadworthy once more. Sepp took 313 in tow until 0100 hrs when we occupied a cornfield for the night and had a few mouthfuls of white wine before retiring. During the night an overzealous sentry shot Gefreiter Saalfelder in the thigh. He had crawled into a haystack and had fallen into such a deep sleep that he failed to respond to the sentry's challenge in the agreed manner by clearing his throat. A towing tractor drove over both of Obergefreiter Dietrich's legs causing flesh wounds but no broken bones.

We arrived at Zelva next evening. We were to have driven up a ramp on to a low-loader of the transporter train. The low-loader, a six-axled Ssyms-wagon, should have been anchored to the rails at its far end but this had been overlooked. As the first Tiger mounted the ramp, the far end tipped up depositing the Tiger on the rails. This destroyed the ramp.

Hagenberger went on to write, 'We then had to load from the side' but here he is evidently confusing it with another incident, for Helmut Küssner recalled this one very clearly. In a reply to Schneider's question Küssner wrote on 22 December 1990:

'You said in your letter something about a report by Hubert Hagenberger to do with loading damaged panzers on the head ramp. This was probably the case in which I was principally involved. Unfortunately I cannot recall the name of the place but it must have been the summer of 1944 because at the time I slept in the open VW. The situation was as follows. After a major operation the workshop platoon had a lot of work on hand with about ten Tigers to repair at the same time. There was no let-up in the Russian pressure so that the CO – at that time still Major Schmidt – ordered the forward workshop platoon to pull back. Therefore I gave the order to get the least damaged panzers operational as soon as possible while the remainder (about six) should proceed alone or with assistance to the nearest workplace. However, the swift Russian advance forced me to choose a workplace much farther back still and I sent these damaged panzers ahead together next day. After we had spent three days without the possibility of setting up a workshop I looked for a railway yard with a head ramp, which would be much farther west particularly since the damaged panzers and I with my staff car were cut off from supply (especially fuel). I found the railway yard (apparently at Zelva) and at once ordered six Ssyms-wagons. I spent almost two days on the telephone. Meanwhile our Tigers had been joined by a half dozen Panthers which were also to be loaded. That went off fairly quickly without a hitch.'

(Hagenberger continues.) Finally, when the Ssyms-wagons arrived, a squad of pioneers were aiming to blow up the station while a colonel of the General Staff wanted to requisition our operational panzers. Thanks be to God I convinced him that none of them was even halfway ready for battle. The loading therefore had to proceed as quickly as possible.

In our haste, contrary to regulations we had not fitted the rail clamps to the Ssyms-wagon so that when the first Tiger drove up the head ramp the loading surface rose, the forward axle slipped out of the pivot pins and rolled away (with the other wagons!) while half the wagon and the panzer finished up on the rails. We acted fast. The locomotive pulled the five wagons clear, and once we had the panzer free of the head ramp we used that in conjunction with railway sleepers for the panzer's fresh ascent, now always using rail clamps for each wagon of course. The mobile panzers drew the 'towed panzers' up the head ramp and I don't believe that the side ramp was used on this loading because we had had bad experiences with the practice in the past.

The panzer transporter had just left the small station when a powerful explosion announced the successful involvement of the pioneers' demolition squad. After that I went to battalion to report to the CO that six damaged Tigers had been got out before the demolition of the station!

(Hagenberger resumes) Everybody heaved a sigh of relief when the transporter (with about thirty vehicles including six Tigers) set off via Volkovysk for Bialystok. After spending a night sleeping in a pine forest I was then summoned by the company commander to drive his command Tiger 300. Oberleutnant Neumeyer had promoted his previous driver, Unteroffizier Georg Ziegeler, a 'parade ground soldier' from Genthin, to panzer commander. Now I was drafted into a new crew, and moreover the command crew, with Funkmeister (senior radio operator) Krug, Unteroffizier Heinz Zinke (gunner) and Fritz Gamsjäger (loader).

After some operations in this area, one day Neumeyer informed the company by radio, 'I am a captain!' Neumeyer, whom we considered fairly young to be of *Hauptmann* rank, had been awarded the German Cross in Gold at Podhorce. After Polonka he had handed me the Iron Cross Second Class of which I was mighty proud, and still am!

Heinz Zinke: 30 July 1944 Augustov

We were in a trough-shaped valley, Augustov being 2 km away on its southern edge. The elongated village was of predominantly small, straw-roofed houses with some barn-type structures. The weather was hot and dry, corresponding to the continental climate. From north of the valley the 'advance of the Red Army' was proceeding, the method being to infiltrate in individual small groups in absolute silence, moving from bush to bush and blending in with the natural surroundings. It was strange how they always managed to be ahead of us, preventing our laying any ambush. Only now and again would we see a head raised above the steppe grass, to disappear the next instant.

Our panzers were facing west with their turrets at three o'clock towards the direction of enemy advance. Suddenly we received Pak fire from the edge of the village. Our panzer was hit several times by 4 cm shells which bored into our armour on the left side but failed to penetrate.

'Turret nine o'clock, HE round!'

We silenced the Pak but also set a house on fire. The flames spread to the straw roofs of the neighbouring houses. Favoured by the hot, dry, easterly wind, soon a sea of flames engulfed the whole village! We had not intended it, but how else could we have defended ourselves?

In the fighting at Augustov on 30 July 1944, radio operator Karl Frischherz from Bruck/Leitha and also Feldwebel Ostermann fell. These hard defensive battles involved heavy losses and were probably the bloodiest in the history of 507 Battalion.

Hubert Hagenberger: The Narew Bridgehead Adventure

The Russians had established a bridgehead over the Narew in the Bialystok area. At first light there was an alert. We had had little sleep for many days, the Russians were breaking through the weak front everywhere and often we managed to repulse an attack only with the most brutal desperation.

Still drunk with sleep I started the panzer engine while the crew cleared off the camouflage. We set off alongside the woods to the *Rollbahn* and then through some small villages apparently resting in peaceful slumber. Above swathes of mist to the east the horizon reddened, heralding sunrise. At the end of one such village was a ford across a swampy stream. I thought that the tracks looked very deep. We crossed safely but once we were in the adjoining meadow with the rising sun in our eyes, Russian tanks attacked from the mist. Our radio aerial was ripped away by a shell or splinter so that our commanding officer lost contact with the company. Therefore he took his files and changed panzers. A few minutes later Unteroffizier Giese came to replace him. The Russian tank force was about eighty strong attacking frontally and from our right flank.

Because the driver knew only a limited amount about a battle, mainly what he heard through his headphones, this time I did not know what was going on. From the talk inside the panzer I was aware that it was getting very lively outside. Giese ordered me to pull back a bit and then we received a hit which broke the left-side track. I jumped down to ascertain the damage and saw the track lying stretched out in the meadow. While I was assessing the possibilities of refitting it a shell hissed by overhead, luckily missing the panzer and convincing me that repair work was out of the question. I re-entered the vehicle to report the situation. Giese said the situation was shit. The radio operator and gunner had made frantic attempts to restore radio contact without success. To make the repair one had to crouch motionless in a small box on the hull where certain death awaited if one became a target.

The race with death could now begin. This was incidentally the first day of battle in which 507 was led by Hauptmann Schöck; very many enemy tanks were destroyed, but we failed to eliminate the bridgehead for lack of infantry. Because our hinterland was swamp, probably for this reason Giese gave the order 'Prepare panzer for destruction'. Of the two Z85 demolition charges, one was laid in the V-shaped trough of the engine between the partition walls, and the other in the open breech in the loading tray of the gun. In this way all panzers which fell into the hands of the enemy would have the same parts destroyed. We all baled out of the panzer into the next nearest. Kurt Lehmann opened his hatch and soon I was sitting behind his seat. After a few seconds we heard a dull report and our abandoned 300 began to burn.

We now had to resolve the difficult question of how to get back over the swampy brook. Its banks were overgrown with alders and bushes and concealed enemy infantry, who would have to be wiped out by the MGs of our Tigers. It was congested at the ford. Julius Quäcke, an innkeeper's son from Neunkirchen/Lower Austria, informed us that Leutnant Lischka was dead and his panzer was sinking into the bog. Unteroffizier Engelhardt had received severe burns from the burst barrel which had killed the commander and loader.

We decided to board. The turret was still projecting above the swamp as we made our way gingerly towards it. Leutnant Rudolf Lischka was in the commander's seat, his head fallen back, face upwards. His blond hair and the skin of his face were burnt. The dead loader lay on the revolving stage, bare from the waist up. Engelhardt, the driver and the radio operator had baled out successfully. Driver Quäcke said that after the explosion he had wanted to save the panzer but had missed the ford and been 'sucked down'. Lehmann, who had gone quite white at hearing this, now headed for the muddy waters of the ford which lay before us, its bed furrowed by numerous vehicles. On the panzer hull a crowd of panzer crews armed with MGs and machine pistols kept up a permanent fire into the bushes on the river bank. When the panzer rose from the waters after the brief crossing of the ford, the sigh of relief was audible! Ivan's artillery was shooting from the village. On the way we picked up panzer commander Unteroffizier Karl Krestau from a cornfield. He was wearing gasmask goggles.

Later we were told that we had destroyed thirty-six of the eighty Russian tanks for the loss of ten of our own, though mainly these were lost due to indirect enemy action, and we had had to retreat. Therefore the Narew Bridgehead Adventure had to go down as a defeat. We moved out towards Chervony-Bor (Red Wood) as far as Lornca. That was probably on 23 August 1944.

From a Main/Franconia Newspaper:
'507 Battalion Sergeant Wins Knight's Cross'

'During the fighting south-west of Bialystok in August 1944, the platoon leader of a panzer company, Fahnenjunker-Oberfeldwebel Rolf Gebhardt, received the order to secure a location with two Tiger tanks. After some time there he noticed a heavily armed Soviet regiment coming up from the east through a valley basin and decided to attack. He drove first to the western end of the valley with both Tigers and destroyed a large part of the enemy force at close range. When a German grenadier battalion then counter-attacked from the west, he detached his second Tiger to support their operation and proceeded, ignoring all danger from nearby woodlands, to the eastern end of the gully where he attacked the Soviet regiment from the rear and wiped it out.

Wie Rolf Gebhardt das Ritterkreuz verdiente

Während der Kämpfe südwestlich Bialystok bekam der Zugführer in einer Panzer-Division, Fhj.-Oberfeldwebel Rolf G e b h a r d t , den Befehl, mit zwei Tigerpanzern einen Ort zu sichern. Als er nach einiger Zeit bemerkte, daß ein sowjetisches Regiment mit allen schweren Waffen von Osten durch eine Talmulde marschierte, entschloß er sich sofort, dieses zu vernichten. Er fuhr zunächst mit beiden Wagen an den Westausgang der Mulde und zerschlug, blitzschnell zupackend, aus nächster Entfernung einen großen Teil des Feindes. Als dann von Westen her ein deutsches Grenadier-Bataillon zum Gegenangriff antrat, gab er diesem zur Unterstützung seinen zweiten Tiger mit und fuhr, selbst ungeachtet aller Bedrohung aus den naheliegenden Waldstücken an den Ostrand der Schlucht. Hier wurde ihm das sowjetische Regiment, wie er es angenommen hatte, vor die Waffen seines Tigers getrieben. In kürzester Frist zerschlug er unter höchstem Einsatz seiner Person das gesamte Regiment mit allen schweren Waffen. Der Führer verlieh dafür dem altbewährten Oberfeldwebel, der seit April 1944 schon 27 Panzer und 36 Geschütze ohne eigene Verluste vernichtete, das Ritterkreuz des Eisernen Kreuzes.

Fhj.-Oberfeldwebel Rolf Gebhardt, der auch das Deutsche Kreuz in Gold trägt, wurde am 19. September 1915 in Karlstadt geboren. Der Vater des Ritterkreuzträgers ist Postinspektor. Seine Familie wohnt heute in Würzburg, Haugerkirchgasse.

Fahnenjunker Oberfeldwebel Rolf Gebhardt was awarded the German Cross in Gold on 28 April and the Knight's Cross on 30 September 1944.

A report on the award of the Knight's Cross to Rolf Gebhardt appeared in the usual way in his local newspaper in Main in Franconia.

Rolf Gebhardt (*left*) as a *Panzerschütze* (private) in late 1937, shortly after joining Panzer Regiment 4, and (*right*) as a *Feldwebel* while on home leave in 1942.

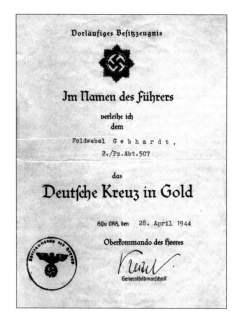
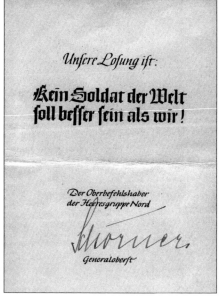

Above left: Award of the German Cross in Gold to Rolf Gebhardt on 28 April 1944. *Above right:* When Rolf Gebhardt was awarded the Knight's Cross the Commander-in-Chief, Army Group North, Generaloberst Schörner, sent this statement of resolve: 'No soldiers in the world will be better than ours!'

VORLÄUFIGES BESITZEUGNIS

DER FÜHRER

HAT DEM

Fhj.Oerfeldwebel Gebhardt ,

Zugf. 2. / Pz. Abt. 5o7

DAS RITTERKREUZ

DES EISERNEN KREUZES

AM 3o.9.1944 VERLIEHEN

HQu OKH, DEN   15.Oktober 1944

OBERKOMMANDO DES HEERES

I.A.

GENERALLEUTNANT

In the defensive actions of the late summer 1944, Fahnenjunker Oberfeldwebel
Rolf Gebhardt distinguished himself to the extent that he was awarded the Knight's
Cross on 30 September 1944 while serving as platoon leader of 2nd Company,
Panzer Battalion 507. This document is the provisional award certificate.

'The Führer has therefore awarded the Knight's Cross of the Iron Cross to this highly proven senior sergeant who since April 1944 has destroyed twenty-seven enemy tanks and thirty-five guns without loss to his own force. Fahnenjunker-Oberfeldwebel Gebhardt, who is also a wearer of the German Cross in Gold, was born at Karlstadt in 1915 and comes from Würzburg.'

Heinz Zinke: Zambrov as I Saw It, 22 August 1944

We had taken up a position with several panzers east of Zambrov. At the foot of a gently rising hill, whose crest we were unable to survey, stood a hamlet of unknown name. It was from there that an enemy tank attack had begun over terrain favourable to the Russians, and in the course of the exchanges we received a hit on the cylindrical mantlet close to the gun. The round had lodged there and was preventing the gun running back after firing. We pulled back allowing Neumeyer to transfer to another panzer. In rolling back we received another hit which tore off a track. Above us enemy bombers were heading for the hinterland.

We had little infantry support. The Russians worked their way forward in groups, almost impossible to observe since the terrain offered the best protection. At the edge of the village to our left, the first enemy groups dug in and took us under fire. Despite the shooting I crawled out to the track and hung it on. Radio operator Kurt Kramer, who had watched my action through his viewing slit, said afterwards, 'I was sure you were a goner there.'

Finally another panzer arrived to tow us out. The hawser was attached but the attempt failed. A counter-shaft of the towing vehicle broke (typical weak point) and so we had no option but to blow up both Tigers. If I remember correctly there was a swampy area in the downhill surface not overlooked by the enemy. When we went back we passed the Tiger of the dead Leutnant Lischka which had suffered a barrel burst.

Heinrich Diez: Memories of Tiger 331

In the operational area Tarnopol–Brody my crew consisted of Kurt Lehmann (driver), Kurt Kramer (radio operator), Helmut Schneider (gunner) and Heinz Seidl (loader). In the Army Group Centre sector Schneider, who left Podhorce for officer cadet school, was replaced by Unteroffizier Dickhoff, and shortly before I went to officer cadet school myself at the end of August, Kramer became the leader-radio operator in Neumeyer's panzer.

Kurt Kramer: In Praise of an 'Old Bones'

In putting together Panzer Battalion 507, 1st and 2nd Companies recruited the majority of their people from veteran panzer crews while for the most part 3rd Company preferred to rely on reinforcements born after 1924 for its leader positions and commanders. Who would be surprised therefore if these nineteen-year-old boys considered that a panzer commander ten years older than them was due for his pension?

In Tiger 313 with Oberfeldwebel Heinrich Diez, leader of 3rd Platoon, 3rd Company, as our commander, as far as we were concerned he was one of the 'old men', in our eyes an old fossil, a little senile, always trying to divert our youthful high spirits along the path of good military discipline. After the first battles in the Tarnopol–Brody area however it became clear to us that in our commander we had actually won the lottery. His battle experience, his circumspection, his calmness exuding confidence and conviction in critical situations, gave us all a feeling of security for which otherwise in those days there was really no justification. 331 seemed vulnerable to every mine which Ivan dug in our path but this did not shake us. In the company, Diez was known as 'Mines-Heini' and soon became mentioned often: of the first twenty-five victories over enemy tanks achieved by 3rd Company, 331 claimed thirteen of them, surely a sign that here one of the smallest battle units functioned like clockwork.

Tarnopol, a sunny day but a thin layer of snow covered the ground. We stood in a security position 500 m from a village where nothing stirred. A lazy day lay ahead. Half left was a wrecked T-34, its cannon turned aside. A Russian came out of a house, leant against the wall in the sun and began picking off his lice. The turret MG shot him dead. Shortly after a second man came through the door without seeing the body of his dead comrade, and he suffered the same fate. While we were discussing the stupidity of these two, the commander ordered, 'Turret half past ten, AP shell on the T-34. Ready. Fire!' Direct hit. While we had been picking off 'harmless individuals', our commander had noticed that the gun of the apparently wrecked T-34 was bearing round towards us. Coming out of its coma, the T-34 was a dangerous animal, and the alertness of the commander had saved us.

A couple of days later we were again on security duty elsewhere. At our back was a large village. Suddenly a round hissed past from the rear, apparently from a Russian Pak. We looked towards the village but nothing was to be seen. A second round was fired, no muzzle flash and missed again. As we heard the explosion Diez turned about and saw where the shell hit. Now he had the line of fire back from that point and above our panzer which

VÖLKISCHER BEOBACHTER

Freitag, 1. September 1944 ● Nr. 245 ● Seite 2

Der Wehrmachtbericht vom Mittwoch

(Für einen Teil der Auflage wiederholt)

Aus dem Führerhauptquartier, 30. August.

Das Oberkommando der Wehrmacht gibt bekannt:

Nachdem unsere Divisionen starke bis zu siebenmal wiederholte Angriffe des Feindes aus seinen Seine-Brückenköpfen nordwestlich Paris in harten Kämpfen aufgefangen hatten, setzten sie sich befehlsgemäß auf neue Stellungen nach Nordosten ab. Die Stadt Rouen wurde nach Zerstörung der Hafenanlagen und sonstiger militärisch wichtiger Objekte aufgegeben.

Zwischen Paris und Reims wurden die nach Norden angreifenden nordamerikanischen Kräfte in erbitterten Kämpfen zum Stehen gebracht. Im Südteil von Soissons sind heftige Straßenkämpfe entbrannt. Südlich der Marne erreichten motorisierte feindliche Verbände im Vorstoß nach Osten die Gegend von Chalons-sur-Marne, um das schwer gekämpft wird.

Im Rhonetal wiesen unsere Flankensicherungen zahlreiche feindliche Angriffe von Osten her ab. Eine größere Anzahl feindlicher Panzer wurde vernichtet.

Im Alpengebiet westlich der französisch-italienischen Grenze wurde die Stadt Briancon nach hartem Kampf mit französischen Terroristen und amerikanischen Aufklärungskräften wieder in Besitz genommen.

Schnellboote versenkten in der Nacht zum 30. August westlich Dieppe einen feindlichen Zerstörer. Im gleichen Seegebiet vernichteten Kampffähren und Sicherungsfahrzeuge der Kriegsmarine einen britischen Zerstörer der Hunt-Klasse, der nach schwerer Detonation auseinanderbrach.

Das V-1-Vergeltungsfeuer auf London dauert an.

In Italien fanden größere Kampfhandlungen nur im adriatischen Küstenabschnitt statt. In den Vormittagsstunden wurden hier heftige Angriffe des Gegners verlustreich für ihn abgewiesen.

In Rumänien scheiterten Angriffe der Sowjets bei Buzau und im Bistrizatal. Die dazwischen über die Pässe des ungarischen Grenzgebietes vorgedrungenen feindlichen Kräfte wurden an mehreren Stellen im Gegenangriff zurückgeworfen. Schlachtfliegerverbände griffen sowjetische Kolonnen auf den Karpatenpässen mit Bomben und Bordwaffen erfolgreich an. Im Weichselbrückenkopf westlich Baranow blieben wiederholt Angriffe der Bolschewisten erfolglos.

Nordöstlich Warschau sowie zwischen Bug und Narew fingen unsere Truppen erneut von Panzern und Schlachtfliegern unterstützte Angriffe der Sowjets in harten Panzerkämpfen auf.

Im Nordabschnitt brachen mehrere Angriffe des Feindes westlich Modohn und nordwestlich Dorpat verlustreich zusammen. In der Nacht waren Truppenansammlungen und Bereitstellungen der Sowjets in den Räumen von Modohn und Dorpat An-

griffsziele unserer Kampf- und Nachtschlachtflieger.

Nordamerikanische Bomber griffen die Städte Mährisch-Ostrau und Oderberg sowie ungarisches Gebiet an. In der Nacht führte die britische Luftwaffe erneut unter Verletzung schwedischen Hoheitsgebietes Terrorangriffe gegen Stettin und Königsberg. Einzelne feindliche Flugzeuge warfen außerdem Bomben auf Berlin und Hamburg.

Luftverteidigungskräfte schossen bei diesen Angriffen 82 viermotorige Terrorbomber ab.

*

Ergänzend zum heutigen OKW.-Bericht wird gemeldet:

Zwischen Bug und Narew haben sich eine Kampfgruppe der 7. Infanteriedivision unter Führung von Oberst Weber und die schwere Panzerabteilung 507 unter Führung des Ritterkreuzträgers Major Schmidt durch unerschütterliche Standfestigkeit und schneidig geführte Gegenstöße besonders ausgezeichnet.

Eine Jagdgruppe unter Führung von Hauptmann Lang schoß im Westkampfraum seit Invasionsbeginn 100 feindliche Flugzeuge ab und zeichnete sich auch bei Tiefangriffen gegen den Feind besonders aus.

In der Bretagne hat eine vom Feind eingeschlossene Stützpunktbesatzung der Luftnachrichtentruppe unter Führung von Oberleutnant Sasse wochenlang schwersten Angriffen weit überlegener Kräfte in heldenhaftem Kampf standgehalten und die viermalige Aufforderung zur Übergabe abgelehnt.

Panzer Battalion 507 led by Major Schmidt was mentioned in the *Wehrmacht Bulletin* of 30 August 1944.

This newspaper article appeared in the *Völkischer Beobachter* on Friday 1 September 1944 at page 2. The indicated paragraph reads: 'Between the Bug and Narew, a battle group of 7th Infantry Division led by Oberst Weber, and Heavy Panzer Battalion 507 led by Knight's Cross holder Major Schmidt, distinguished itself especially by its unshakable steadfastness and spirited counter-attacks.'

---

led to a barn with a door panel missing. Schneider's HE shell tore the door to shreds and exposed behind it 'our' Pak.

At dusk, the Tigers of our company were driving two abreast through a long village. Company commander Fritz Neumeyer occupied the position 20 m ahead to our right. Close to our left stood the last house. Apart from distant MG fire there were no sounds of resistance to be heard, nor anything we could see which might have given Diez reason to traverse the turret to nine o'clock. Neumeyer, looking ahead, had already passed the last house and as we drew beyond it we saw an enemy tank aiming at Neumeyer's panzer. Our fast, close-range round blew up the enemy tank. After the operation, Neumeyer came over with a great pack of cigarettes and pressed them into our hands without speaking.

Just by chance, in turning on a spot, our Tiger had unearthed a giant bone from the earth of Galicia. Lacking training in palaeontology we were unable to determine whether it came from a dinosaur or a local camel. Either way we preserved it carefully in order to present it to Diez on his 30th birthday (Podhorce, 22 June 1944), and then celebrated in the tower. An old bone for an 'Old Bones'.

A few days later we loaded up for the Army Group Centre sector, and straight from the ramp at Baranovicze set off for our new operational area. The line of Tigers threw up massive clouds of dust which not only stung the eyes and burned the throat but also lay millimetre-thick on equipment and weapons, not good for sensitive MGs.

3rd Platoon veered away from the direction of advance to protect the flanks northwards. In a large field of maize 2 m tall the gunner had little chance, and the driver or radio operator even less, of seeing anything. The commander could see 360° but only above the tops of the maize plants. Whole regiments could hide themselves in these fields.

From higher up in the cupola, Diez saw two Russian assault guns which we destroyed. At the edge of a field of maize where it grew more thinly the outline of a Pak became visible (later found to be a US-supplied 9.2 cm gun). It had been tracking the engine noise of our neighbour but then traversed its aim to us.

'Gun and MG, fire at will!' Diez shouted. Nothing happened. Stoppage on all weapons, probably clogged up, the worst that could happen in this situation.

'Ram, Lehmann!' Diez ordered and, standing in the turret, began shooting with his pistol at the Pak gunners. The Tiger bounded forward, after which Diez attempted to engage the Pak with hand grenades. About 15 m short of the collision, the Russian anti-tank gun fired again but to no avail, the Tiger kept rolling and seconds later Lehmann rammed the Pak barrel which contorted, and crushed the splayed outriggers. The Pak crew fled into the maize. How they had managed to miss us twice at such short range remains a mystery. Yet such wonders rarely happen by themselves. The commander's understanding of the situation and speed of reaction were definitely major factors in unnerving the enemy Pak crew.

In the course of the defensive fighting north-west of Sniadov (Army Group Centre sector), 3rd Platoon was detached to support an infantry unit under heavy pressure. Since they had no ammunition, we gave them some of our MG belts. While doing this there came the shout, 'Enemy tanks from the right!' – apparently Josef Stalins. Lightning-fast came our reaction and we destroyed two of them within seconds. When our 8.8 cm gun fired again, Diez fell as if struck by lightning from the turret cupola into the vehicle, his forehead bleeding.

'Commander is dead!' somebody shouted.

'Commander is alive,' the calm voice of Diez replied. When the gun recoiled, our panzer had jerked back a hand's breadth (that is to say the tracks teetered). As a consequence of this movement a Russian sniper's bullet only grazed his forehead!

That operation was to have been my last with Oberfeldwebel Diez, for meanwhile I had been nominated to take over in the company commander's panzer as radio operator. 3rd Company stood at readiness at the edge of a wood. The commander, Oberleutnant Neumeyer, was in conference with the CO. He had given orders that should an action develop suddenly, his deputy should take over but whatever the circumstances the crew of his own panzer should stand by and wait for him. ('I'm not having my own crew shot to pieces.')

Suddenly the order came down to intercept and destroy twelve enemy tanks heading for our main battle line. Diez was apparently not happy with the new man assigned to him as his driver, came over to me and asked, 'Will you?' I agreed, disobeying the express order of Leutnant Neumeyer. Our platoon rolled across our battle line protecting its left flank, but then we came under heavy fire from woodlands to our left which posed us a difficult problem.

Diez found partial cover in a depression but his request to the deputy company leader twice repeated to deal with the threat on our own flank was ignored: 'Diez, fall back at once, that is an order!' Up until that point, apart from our panzer the company had had no contact with the enemy. So we drew back. Scarcely had we shown ourselves over the reverse slope than we received a fierce cannonade which resulted in immediate damage to the lateral counter-shaft causing the panzer to proceed in a circle. It was only a matter of time before the next hit arrived and so, 'Bale out!' We jumped down into a potato field, the commander's fall softened by the back of a Russian. Seconds later the panzer was hit again and again and began to burn.

The potato field offered such good cover that despite enemy infantry and even Pak fire we got far enough away for Diez to explain his plan of escape, which was for each of us to make his way back individually to a haystack in

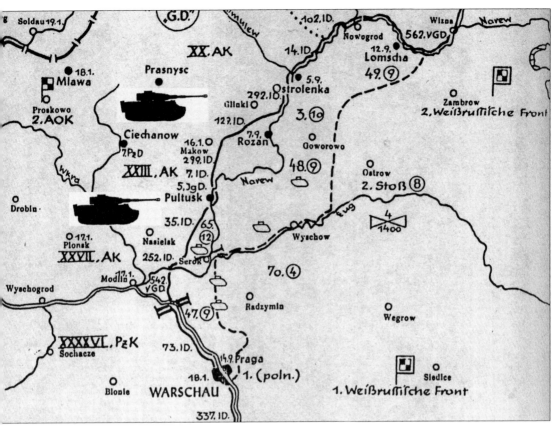

This map shows the line of retreat followed by 507 Battalion to Nasielsk and Zichenau, autumn 1944.

the distance where we would be safe. However, despite heavy fire, a Tiger came towards us at full speed: Claus-Peter Müller's 334 brought us out of the danger zone, dropped us at the haystack and then carried on forwards.

Now another Tiger came up from the rear, the command panzer of Lieutenant Neumeyer. He waved aside my stammered apology for disobeying his order with the words, 'Get in, I'm just happy that you're still alive!' For the first time I realised what Neumeyer meant by his earlier remark; he identified so closely with his crew that he did not want to trust their lives to anybody else.

Heinrich Diez was sent off to officer cadet training shortly after this episode and received his commission before the war ended. He managed to conceal his German Cross in Gold from all searchers during captivity and brought it home. With the exception of Kurt Lehmann, who fell later in the command panzer, all members of Diez's first Tiger crew in 331 survived the war, captivity and the early post-war era. As pensioners, gunner Helmut Schneider, loader Hans Seidl, radio operator Kurt Kramer and I still recall in thankful remembrance the close ties we had to our commander.

Kurt Kramer: The Great Fluke Shot

I can vouch for the truth of the following story. Somewhere in open country a pair of Tigers stood on security duty. With the exception of the watchkeepers, the crews were inside their panzers. Six to eight kilometres away was a *Rollbahn* controlled by the Russians. The whole terrain was flat and easily surveyed and so no great watchfulness was necessary. In one of the Tigers was gunner Obergefreiter Franz Dietrich from Nienburg/Weser. He was seated at his sights looking at the view when suddenly he saw a convoy of lorries escorted by a single tank appear at the far end of the *Rollbahn*. The range of nearly 8 km was far beyond the effective range of an 8.8 cm KwK gun, but Dietrich thought that there would be no harm in trying a 'pot shot', however, and obtained permission from the commander.

The loader took a single armour-piercing shell from the supports and pushed it into the breech. The sliding block fell. 'Clack!' Dietrich now realised how tiny the target was in the sights. To fire over such a range required indirect aim with elevation, but to have the gun pointing that high obstructed the view through the sight! Therefore he lowered the barrel in order to aim, allowed 200 to 300m for lateral deflection, raised the barrel again and fired! The shell rose high into the blue sky.

The length of time it took that 8.8cm shell to cover 8 km on whatever trajectory it happened to be flying is not known but myth has it that Franz was able to borrow some tobacco, fill his pipe with it, borrow a lighter and then take a few puffs before he saw the spectacular result of his gunnery and shouted aloud his success.

The crew, speechless, tore open the hatches and saw in the far distance, where once the Soviet tank had been, a cloud of black smoke through which streaks of fire flashed. The plunging shell had been a direct hit. The incident was observed by other Tiger crews and confirmed officially.

Chapter 5

THE BATTLE FOR THE NAREW BRIDGEHEADS

Once the Russians had begun their offensive in Army Group Centre's sector on 22 June 1944, the Red Army's advance, despite bitter defensive fighting and the occasional counter-attack, had proceeded so efficiently that its forward units established a number of small bridgeheads over the River Narew, as for example at Szelkov and Serock, which they attempted to expand and merge during the course of the next few months.

Panzer Battalion 507 was deployed here until November 1944, either as reserve, in action or on security duty. On 4 October heavy fighting broke out in which the German objective of destroying the Narew bridgeheads was not achieved although limited successes were obtained, at times in cooperation

A tripod-mounted MG42 in a defensive position ready for the next attack.

with Panzer Battalion 509. In the fighting on 5 October 1944, 3rd Company Commander, recently promoted Hauptmann Fritz Neumeyer, fell.

In August 1944, 507's commanding officer, Major Erich Schmidt, had been transferred out to take command of a panzer regiment of the Führergrenadier-Brigade. Hauptmann Fritz Schöck became the new commanding officer, having been commander of 2nd Company. Oberleutnant Georg Reinhardt was appointed as the new adjutant, transferred in from Panzer Battalion 509 to replace Oberleutnant Wolf Koltermann.

The other changes at company level were as follows:

1st Company: Hauptmann Holzheid was transferred to a supply battalion and replaced by Oberleutnant Rudi Beilfuss, former leader 1st Platoon, 1st Company.

2nd Company: Hauptmann Schöck was replaced by the former leader of 1st Platoon, 2nd Company, Max Wirsching.

3rd Company: Following the death in action of Hauptmann Neumeyer, his replacement was the former adjutant, Oberleutnant Wolf Koltermann.

The entries for 'operational days' in the *Soldbuch* of Leutnant Gerd Eychmüller confirm him as leader of 1st Platoon, 1st Company: see also diary entries for Erwin Aichinger (Staff Company), Anton Seefried and Siegfried Obermayr (A Company).

Calendar and Diary Entries

25 September 1944
SEEFRIED: I drove from the military hospital at Praschnitz to Zichenau and then on to Mielau where I went to the cinema and spent the night at the Wehrmacht hostel.

27 September 1944
SEEFRIED: I was sent by the *Frontleitstelle* to Nasielsk and joined 2nd Company. From there a horse-drawn wagon brought me to the staff echelon in a wood near Vinnica.

When the Soviets set foot in Reich territory for the first time in East Prussia
in the late summer of 1944, work on erecting defences had begun so late
that they ultimately proved useless.

28 September 1944

SEEFRIED: At 1400 hrs I went with the Senior Paymaster to the *Tross* for a few days' convalescence.

1 October 1944

AICHINGER: We are at Chroscice. We have to destroy a Russian bridgehead west of the Narew.

2 October 1944

OBERMAYR: Russian attack at the Narew.

3 October 1944

OBERMAYR: Fighting at the bridgehead.

4 October 1944

OBERMAYR: Fighting at the bridgehead.

EYCHMÜLLER: North of Serock, Trzepov.

5 October 1944

AICHINGER: Hauptmann Neumeyer fell.

OBERMAYR: Hauptmann Neumeyer fell.

EYCHMÜLLER: Dzierzenin.

6 October 1944

EYCHMÜLLER: Dzierzenin.

7 October 1944

EYCHMÜLLER: Height 108.

8 October 1944

EYCHMÜLLER: South of Niestepov.

9 October 1944

EYCHMÜLLER: South-east of Niestepov.

SEEFRIED: I went to the command post and attended the burial of Unter-offizier Lachner who fell on 8 October. Hauptmann Fritz Neumeyer is buried there too. On the following day we left the Vinnica woods, giving our fallen

Unteroffizier Scheuerlein (*right*) on Tiger 231 with an unidentified comrade.
The Zimmerit anti-limpet mine coating can be seen to good effect.

comrades a last salute as we passed their graves. On our journey towards
Mackeim we were attacked by *Jabos*.

11 October 1944

EYCHMÜLLER: North of Las.

SEEFRIED: At the support point as radio post.

12 October 1944

EYCHMÜLLER: Chrzanov, south of Pluscz.

OBERMAYR: Russians broke through.

SEEFRIED: Nothing special to report,

13 October 1944

EYCHMÜLLER: Probostvo and Soye.

OBERMAYR: We are west of Mackeim.

SEEFRIED: We went into another wood from where at 0945 hrs we had to go forward with the commanding officer. On the way the Cardan shaft broke. We are at Bloniavi, Carli is radioing the support point for help.

14 October 1944

SEEFRIED: Towards midday a towing tractor arrived from the recovery platoon. It already had Feldwebel Rühl's SPW in tow. Rühl, Fischer and Redl are all seriously wounded. We were towed to the repair unit where both vehicles were made operational within 48 hours.

EYCHMÜLLER: We are on Height 107 south of Cziezielov.

15 October 1944

EYCHMÜLLER: Height 107, east side Yakliczev

17 October 1944

SEEFRIED: We drove to the support point where I took over the radio connection to Battalion, which is engaged in heavy fighting at Rozan on the Narew.

18 October 1944

AICHINGER: Poor quarters at Grudus. Obergefreiter Pospichal assigned as Writer.

SEEFRIED: I spent all day until midnight at the radio set.

19 October 1944

EYCHMÜLLER: Yakliczev and Height 109.

SEEFRIED: I resumed at the radio set at 0400 hrs and at 1000 hrs took down a message stating that the enemy has taken a village which we must recapture in a counter-attack.

20 October 1944

SEEFRIED: I was relieved by Zemann at the radio because we have to take provisions and ammunition forward during the night.

21 October 1944

SEEFRIED: There is a lull.

24 October 1944

EYCHMÜLLER: Boby, west and south-west of Boby.

25 October 1944

EYCHMÜLLER: West of Boby.

OBERMAYR: We are stationed near a *Grossdeutschland* Panther unit.

26 October 1944

EYCHMÜLLER: Eastwards of Glodov.

7 November 1944

OBERMAYR: We are at Zabin-Karnievski, 2 km from Karnievo.

8 November 1944

OBERMAYR: Saw *Frau Luna* in the cinema at Karnievo.

Gerd Eychmüller: Impressions of Sixteen Days of Operations

After approximately two months of defensive battles in Army Group Centre's sector, we had so dampened down the Russians' strength that at first they gave up the idea of launching out from their two strong bridgeheads at Rozan and Nasielsk on the Narew River north of Warsaw. Panzer Battalion 507 was therefore able to spend four weeks recuperating from the strain of fighting these endless retreats, and to 'lick its wounds'. As I recall, a large section of the battalion laid up in a sparse wood which was soon converted into an assembly area for very substantial numbers of our troops. It was there that I got to see the 'King Tiger' for the first time with which the newly formed Panzer Battalion 505 had been equipped.[1]

On 4 October 1944 we began the attempt to crush, and if possible eliminate entirely, the bridgeheads on the River Narew. That day the Tiger of my company commander, Oberleutnant Beilfuss, was hit, killing the driver while the commander himself was seriously wounded and had to be transported

---

1. The King Tiger, Pz.Kpfw. VI Ausf. B, Sd.Kfz. 182, Tiger II, differed from the Tiger I by its weight, 68 tonnes as against 55 tonnes, mainly because of its thicker armour (maximum 185mm as against 110 mm). It also had a more powerful 8.8 cm KwK 43 L/71 gun (an improvement on the KwK L/56).

to military hospital. As a result I was called upon to take charge of 1st Company, an unexpected task for which I was unprepared. From my *Soldbuch* entries I see that this attack occurred north of Serock, that is in the sector of the Nasielsk bridgehead. There now followed five full days of operations, details of which I no longer remember except that on 5 October my former commander in 3rd Company, Hauptmann Neumeyer, lost his life. 1st Company lost platoon leader Oberfeldwebel Zulauf, his driver and gunner, to a Pak hit. Feldwebel Weber (panzer commander, 1st Platoon) was killed when a round from a SU-152 self-propelled gun tore off the turret of his panzer.

That the aforementioned six days of battle (the last was my 23rd birthday) not only involved heavy casualties but were also extraordinarily tiring can be seen by the fact that during an attack made by our company on a broad front as part of a larger unit, I fell asleep in my commander's seat and only awoke when my gunner, who must have noticed how silent I had become, gave my left leg a strong shaking!

The numerous mines sown by the Russians to complicate our penetration of their bridgeheads caused us great vexation. I can still picture myself and my crew on our knees stabbing into the ground with long metal rods trying to locate mines and render them harmless. Nevertheless my panzer was not spared running over these evil things: twice they knocked us out with track damage. Such repairs as were possible with the tools we carried aboard were always nerve-wracking. Apart from the heavy labour involved, repairs were not only carried out under the pressure of time, but occasionally also in the greatest danger, for mined areas were almost always under enemy fire whose purpose in being there was to finish off 'the lame ducks'.

In connection with mines, whose explosions permanently damaged my rather sensitive hearing,

In October 1944, 2nd Company's Tiger 203 was with the surplus panzer stock.

I remember that a panzer of my platoon (or in any case of 1st Company) whose gun muzzle was about two metres behind my turret hatch fired a round while I was surveying the area with binoculars. The sudden tremendous noise and air pressure threw me back into my seat, perforated my left eardrum, made me completely deaf for several hours and condemned me to live evermore in the world of the 'hard of hearing'.

After that six-day spell of operations I was given a rest day, followed by another five-day spell of combat, my last two days as recorded in my *Soldbuch* being west and south-west of Boby on 24 October and east of Glodov on the 26th. To my relief, on 29 October Oberleutnant Beilfuss returned from military hospital and resumed command of 1st Company. Even though we and the other units with which we were deployed failed to crush the Narew bridgeheads, and despite our fairly high losses in men and material, we inflicted such heavy casualties on the enemy that for the remainder of 1944 he decided not to attempt to advance any farther westwards.

Kurt Kramer: Hauptmann Neumeyer's Last Day

Decades after the lost war there is so much we have forgotten or repressed. We found that there have been more important things to do than write up the past. In addition, today we see much from another angle, that is to say from the perspective of men of pensionable age, who remain amazed that they survived those events which broke over their untroubled youth. Certain events are stored in our memories with astounding clarity, those which cheered us in dour times, others because they haunt us still for having robbed us of a part of the 'protective shield of comradeship'. I refer now to one of the latter.

On the evening of 5 October 1944, 3rd Company had taken up a position on the edge of a wood. Our mission was to prevent expansion of the bridgehead which the Russians had built at Nasielsk (near Rozan) across the Narew River in an approximately north-easterly direction. Before us lay a slight downward slope which provided a good view. In the distance, half-hidden behind a rise in the ground, was a village, and down there too was sure to be an anti-tank ditch. Of the enemy there was no sign, all we heard of him was light artillery fire coming from the distance. Everything pointed to a quiet night.

Radio silence was in force. This meant that radio operators had to maintain a listening watch and not transmit except in an emergency. Shortly before,

Crew of the Tiger commanded by Feldwebel Ludwig Scheuerlein
on 1 October 1944. The photo provides a good view of the rubber-saving
steel running wheels on the final version of the Tiger I.

Feldwebel Ludwig Scheuerlein (*left*) with his men by the massive front of the Tiger I. It was usual for Tigers of 507 to have spare track segments attached at the level of the viewing ports as extra armour protection.

we had been able to hear the Russians on our frequency which meant that they could probably hear us. This was also the reason why the company commander had gone on foot that evening to give the platoon leaders their last instructions for the night. Because the command panzer was non-operational, I had transferred into another panzer with Hauptmann Fritz Neumeyer, as was customary for the senior radio operator, and I was now waiting with the rest of the crew for the commander's return.

Fritz Neumeyer belonged amongst those officers who could command a unit with a 'light touch'. With him, conversation had precedence over an order, and the homogeneous co-operation within the company was more important to him than the constant demonstration of his power of command. Undoubtedly his upbringing played a major role: raised in Berlin, he brought with him the cheerfulness, the easy manner and the amiable charm of his home region which, together with his own calmness and the certainty he radiated, were for him the fundamental principles of command.

I became very irritated when, in the absence of the commander and despite radio silence, the completely unencrypted words of a senior officer came over the ether saying that the leader of a certain infantry assault group 'wanted to speak to the commander of 3rd Company'. I began jamming the frequency at once but the most important part of what he had to convey had already been broadcast! The said officer, a major as I recall, was brought to our panzer on foot where Hauptmann Neumeyer had arrived meanwhile.

The major reported that during the early evening Russian infantry had infiltrated the village ahead of us and he intended forcing them out in a single night attack. For this purpose he was requesting the support of our unit. Neumeyer deliberated for some time. All panzer men knew how risky such night attacks could be, for we could see little but be easily seen. The large moving target of a panzer offered a fine opportunity to well-camouflaged anti-tank defences at night. At the urging of the major, Neumeyer finally decided to provide the protection requested, but not the whole company on account of the risk.

The crew enjoying a couple of days' rest at Zichenau where the Workshop Company overhauled many of the battalion's panzers.

Unteroffizier Ludwig Scheuerlein, awarded the Iron Cross First Class in February 1943. As a panzer commander with 2nd Company, on a single day in January 1945 he shared in the destruction of fourteen Russian tanks with Feldwebel Ebner.

On 3 March 1945 Feldwebel Ludwig Scheuerle was awarded the Ehrenblatt Clasp (*inset top left in picture*, roughly equivalent to a mention in dispatches in the Allied forces) to mark his successes in the field.

So far as I recall there were only two or three panzers which felt their way slowly forward through the darkness under Neumeyer's command. He was leaning well forward out of his hatch while I also stood up through my hatch so as to spot any obstacles in the terrain or signs of the enemy. Soon we reached the anti-tank ditch. It was only 2.5 m deep but had very steep sides. As it was impossible to cross the gap we veered right and drove alongside the ditch in the hope of finding a crossing point. This course of action showed the enemy our side profile. Everything remained quiet, however, and the tension in the panzer gradually lessened. After several hundred metres we found a place where the ditch had not been completed, crossed to the other side and drove back to opposite the point from where we had made the detour. Then we turned right again and headed on course for the unseen village in the darkness.

Because of our now assumed proximity to the Russians I had meanwhile resumed my seat but when I glanced back I noticed Neumeyer still standing up in the turret. Over the intercom I suggested he should lower his head a little. 'No worries!' he laughed back, 'I'll be paid for it in the end.' These were the last words he ever spoke. In the same instant we saw muzzle flashes ahead. The fire was well aimed. The shells howled close by the panzer and then a light bump told us that the armour had been 'grazed'. Judging by the brief lapse of time between the hiss of the passing projectiles and the audible report of the gun being fired it was clear that we had come devilish close to an enemy anti-tank position. Before we had time to react there came another, harder blow and a rain of fire pattered through the open turret hatch into the tank. The body of Fritz Neumeyer collapsed and tipped head-first onto the floor of turret. 'Commander dead!' the gunner shouted. A shell had hit the cupola and sheared off the mount for the anti-aircraft machine gun, which had then inflicted a hideous injury on Neumeyer, killing him instantly. There were no other casualties.

As the senior NCO I now took command and ordered an immediate pulling back in order to get crew and panzer out of the danger zone. The driver (Schmidt) did not react at first, perhaps the intercom was temporarily out. Not until I gave him a blow in the back with a hammer did he 'get the message' and finally we rolled back, still under fire. Then abruptly my fatal error became apparent! Under the pressure of events and in the excitement I had quite forgotten that there was an anti-tank ditch to our rear somewhere. In the split second when I remembered it, it was already too late and with a hard jolt the Tiger tipped backwards into the ditch causing everything not lashed down, including all the shells and not least the crew, to whirl about in a heap.

Fortunately nobody was injured. The panzer now rested on its tail fairly steeply upright, a good part of the lightly armoured bottom of the hull inviting the enemy to finish it off. I gave orders to evacuate the panzer since efforts to move it proved fruitless. For some reason best known to themselves, the Russians now ceased firing their anti-tank guns, replacing them with rather wild MG fire. This gave us the chance to get the dead commander out, and using a tarpaulin we dragged him away to our side of the ditch.

Having returned to company in a state of collapse, I was immediately ordered to return to the panzer and blow it up. Oberfeldwebel Hohenwarter saw how exhausted we were and his objection was accepted so that somebody else got the job. I still thank him for that today. Oberleutnant Wolf

Koltermann, the CO's former adjutant, had returned to battalion on 5 October from a company commander's course and took over 3rd Company that same night.

In a Polish birch forest bathed in autumn sunlight we took leave of our much-loved commander with military honours. The commanding officer of 507 Battalion led the last salute. Fritz Neumeyer was laid to rest in the local cemetery at Neidenburg. I had the opportunity later to restore his grave to a worthier condition. A friendly farmer lent me some tools and provided flowers. A short time afterwards, the war broke over East Prussia. My hopes of revisiting the cemetery after the war could not be realised because of the political circumstances then prevailing.

Kurt Kramer: Panzer Battle, with Live Commentary by Radio

Young lieutenants transferred into the battalion did not always have it easy. Now and again one would be drafted to the Staff group so that the commanding officer could look him over. Therefore Leutnant X, for example, who had immediately been appointed a panzer commander, remained under the wing of the battalion commander before being entrusted with a platoon.

In radio traffic between the battalion staff and companies it was the practice to use code names for persons and the turret number for the panzer contacted. The following interesting event could be overheard by a company commander's vehicle whose radio equipment was on the battalion frequency. I shall assign the following code names for the three-way communication: *Schwalbe* = Battalion; *Rose* = Company; *004* = the Tiger of Leutnant X.

The battalion was occupying a position on a plateau where it had a security assignment to watch to the east. The terrain sloped downwards to the south-east and into a valley out of our sight. Reconnaissance of this valley was necessary and the following radio messages were passed accordingly:

> *Schwalbe to 004*
> Drive forward and make observations in the valley in front of you.

> *004 to Schwalbe*
> Understood. I am driving forward.

After a few minutes, very hastily: 'Enemy tanks! Enemy tanks!'

> *Schwalbe to 004*
> Understood. Open fire on them.

Scheurlein's crew at work barrel-cleaning.

Fine interior view of the radio operator's position in the Tiger I. To the left are two bags of ammunition belts alongside the gasmask canister. Above this is a reserve Kinon armoured optic. Top right can be seen the swivel-periscope eyepieces with rubber surrounds.

004 to Schwalbe
There are thirteen!

Schwalbe to 004
Understood. Fire on them!

004 to Schwalbe
I repeat, there are thirteen tanks!

Schwalbe to 004
We understand you. Shoot at them!

Ahead it now grew very quiet. We held our breath. What was our otherwise so cautious CO up to? Surely he wasn't trying to force the poor lieutenant to do something reckless? Soon the next message followed.

Schwalbe to 004

Pull back at once!

Schwalbe to Rose

Leader Rose, take command of Schwalbe. Leader Schwalbe proceeding ahead and signing off.'

What did all this mean? After a period of quiet we heard fifteen to twenty easily recognisable 8.8 cm rounds being fired, dull explosions occurring between each. Then came another message:

Schwalbe to everybody

Schwalbe reporting back and taking command. Thirteen enemy tanks destroyed!

The young lieutenants did not have it easy, and so the 'criticism of their handling of a situation' by radio was discontinued forthwith!

Heinz Stracke: Memoirs of Action with 3rd Company

I was at Podhorce with the first batch of reinforcements from Paderborn for 3rd Company and transferred a few days later with the battalion to the Army Group Centre sector. After a couple of days in which some T-34s were destroyed, the young crew could claim to be 'experienced'.

On another operation in sandy terrain a track of our Tiger jammed. We had to get out and attempt to remove it with explosives. It was the right-hand track and as radio operator I vacated my position and removed everything which might be endangered by the explosion: MG ammunition, radio equipment, provisions box, radio code tables, etc. After this was completed, hand grenades were placed on the track and ignited. We jumped into cover. After the smoke had cleared we saw that the track had survived intact but we now had a hole in the hull which had not been there before. This should have been foreseeable, for the hand grenades needed to have a shield above them such as segments of track or packed earth. Two panzers had stood guard during this activity, and as the repairs staff had now arrived all went well; the workshop people welded over the hole and we rolled out.

Another time we were near a village under continuous Russian artillery fire. We had to shift our position repeatedly to avoid being hit. Despite that they got us. The shell made a strange noise but our luck held for the dud came to rest between the gun and the radio operator's hatch. As a result we lost electrical lighting, probably because the fuse had burnt out. The replacement fuse restored interior lighting and the ventilator began sucking out the bluish-yellow smoke. Nevertheless we had to go back to get the gun adjusted while the bolt for the radio operator's hatch had jammed so firmly that it required a large hammer and crowbar to open it.

A panzer track is only as strong as it weakest link! This truism was confirmed one day when the last panzer of a column was crossing the bed of a small river with a steep slope on its far bank. The warning came by radio: 'Stop at once, your right track will soon part, has received damage!' Our driver Gerhard Schwarz said he would proceed slowly and steadily. In this way we reached the slope, ascended and found a safe spot to change two sections of the track of which more than half had been shot away. Here the 'weakened track' had been 'strong enough'. Gerhard Schwarz fell later at Zichenau when we were no longer together.

After a mission we returned to the assembly area where we had plenty to keep us occupied: refuelling, re-ammunitioning, collecting rations, cleaning weapons, caring for our panzers, etc. Our gunner, Otto Ledermüller, noticed a small gap between the running wheels and began poking inside with a stick. We gave it a closer look. It was about 2–3 cm in diameter and went through the whole thickness of the hull wall. After clearing away shells and debris inside, deep down in the hull we found the steel core projectile of a rifle-grenade. This had penetrated the 60 mm armour of the lower hull!

On an operation I served as radio operator in the Tiger of Oberfeldwebel Diez, leader of 3rd Platoon, 3rd Company. Ledermüller was gunner, Horvat loader. We had been given new steel-cored ammunition for our MG. When the MG was suddenly needed, I reported 'Target recognised' and received permission to fire. After one round the MG refused, and the same happened with the turret MG. Following the report 'MG jammed', the barrel was changed, but without effect. I still had some belts of the previous issue of ammunition which I then loaded and fired normally. The steel-cored projectiles had jammed so tight in the barrel that when they were ejected, the base of the cartridge case was torn away.

Fritz Schreiber: My Cap Flew Off

One evening we were driving with two or three panzers at top speed through burning Bialystok. It was dark and only the flames of the burning houses illuminated the streets. This drive was nearly the death of me. I was leaning out of the turret when suddenly my cap was torn from my head. The cause was a cable or telephone wire strung low across the street. Ten centimetres lower at that speed and it would have cut my throat. A little later, also at night, while driving through a village we received aimed rifle fire, apparently from partisans. I had to leave the turret and crouch down outside the panzer behind the driver's hatch so as not to offer my silhouette for target practice!

Scheuerlein's crew making comments on the last stages of work on a drive wheel.
Zichenau, October 1944.

Chapter 6

A RESTING PLACE AT
ZICHENAU-MIELAU

During November 1944, the Eastern Front came to a gradual standstill. In the northern sector where Panzer Battalion 507 was involved, the front ran along the River Narew to its confluence with the Bug and Vistula near Warsaw, but the two bridgeheads which the Russians had established at Rozan and Nasielsk could not be crushed.

In this area, XXIII Army Corps with 7th, 129th, 299th Infantry Divisions and 5th Jäger Division formed the southern wing of Second Army under Generaloberst Weiss. What we had facing us on the other side or, better put, what was brewing up over there between November and mid-January 1945, could only be guessed at. The supreme leadership was much better informed through General Gehlen's 'Foreign Armies East' intelligence network, the usual reconnaissance reports made locally, and by the sad certainty that the collapse of the Eastern Front in the summer of 1944 had not happened by accident.

Hitler rejected all reasonable suggestions from his army commanders, however, dismissing the reports on enemy strength as 'filthy lies' and the fear that the Russians were capable of a major offensive as 'idiotic'. He also refused to listen to General Guderian, whom he had appointed Chief of the Army General Staff in July 1944 and who had been quoted as comparing the Eastern Front to a house of cards: 'If the front is penetrated at a single place, it will collapse!'

The soldier in the field had felt for some time that the Eastern Front was like a growing child's shirt: too short at the back if you pulled it down at the front, and vice-versa. That this was the bitter truth after the Normandy Invasion became much more obvious when we heard the Special Announcement of the Ardennes Offensive on the evening of 16 December 1944. It sounded promising that Sixth SS Panzer Army (Dietrich), Fifth Panzer Army (Manteuffel) and Seventh Army (Brandenburger), supported by 1,700 aircraft, were participating in such an offensive, but it was also clear to

A German foxhole on the foggy front, winter 1944–5.

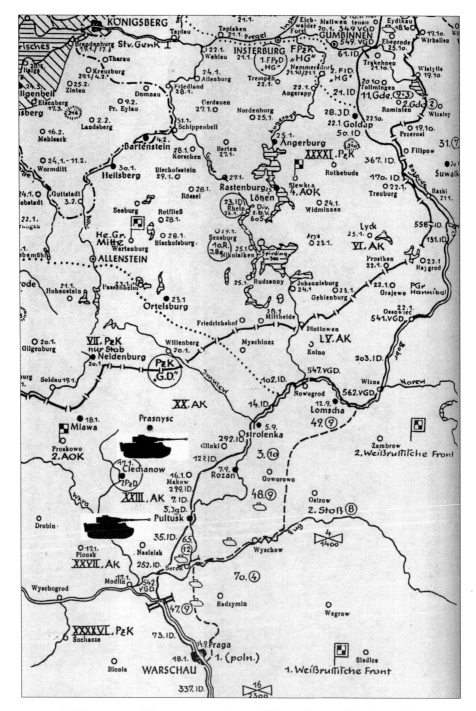

Military map of the operational area of Heavy Panzer Battalion 507,
late 1944–early 1945.

us that these twenty-eight divisions would now be missing from the Eastern Front. Knowing this, our belief in 'Final Victory' received another blow, though the will to fight continued unbroken. The important thing was to protect the Reich against the Russians, while at all costs avoiding the danger of falling into their hands.

Panzer Battalion 507 lay at this time with remnants of 7th Panzer Division as the only army reserve in the Zichenau–Mackeim area which could hold out into the 'winter pause' immediately behind the bridgehead built by the Russians across the River Narew at Szelkov. It was located as follows:

The *Battalion Staff* at the agricultural estate of Mosaki.

1st Company (Oberleutnant Beilfuss) at Bogate as a kind of stiffening behind 299th Infantry Division.

2nd Company (Oberleutnant Wirsching) south of Mosaki.

3rd Company (Oberleutnant Koltermann), which had spent some time at Slasy Slotki, was now at the farmstead of Helenov, north of Mosaki.

Supply Company (Hauptmann Müller) mainly at the Vroblev estate.

Workshop Company W1 (Oberleutnant Küssner) at Paluki, W2 (Oberleutnant Steinborn) at Grzybov, north-west of Zichenau.

From sober reflection on the situation it was clear that in these two months the entire battalion had no choice but to bring panzers, wheeled vehicles, weapons and reinforcements to the highest state of readiness while allowing for rest and recuperation.

Calendar and Diary Entries
Erwin Aichinger

9 November 1944
Memorial Day for the Fallen was held at a farmstead at Grudusk together with Panzer-Jäger Battalion 560.

17 November 1944

Savati Torsky. Further changes in personnel made to economise on manpower.

20 November 1944

I have now been made Supply Company clerk. Hauptfeldwebel Enke is being transferred from Staff Company to the Workshop Company. Oberleutnant Heesch is also being exchanged.

22 November 1944

I am with the Supply Company at Milev Debki.

24 November 1944

Drove to Vroblev on poor, muddy field paths. Then I have leave for Christmas and the New Year.

Leutnant Dieter Jähn

17 October 1944

End of the gunnery instructor's course at Putlos. Returned to Reserve Battalion 500, Paderborn (Unit 'Black'), which is the core for the formation of the new Panzer Battalion 513 transferred to Bentfeld (west of Paderborn).

27 October 1944

Submitted the gunnery manual I have written: 'Enlargement and Commentary on Army Service Regulations 470/20 with Regard to Panzer Gun 43 in the Tiger B'. Now I have leave until 10 November 1944.

10 November 1944

I have been drafted to Panzer Battalion 507.

15 November 1944

Leutnant Gustl Stadler and I each took over one transport train with six Tigers.

21 November 1944

Arrival at Zichenau after the train was diverted via Ortelsburg (!) I have been introduced to officers of Battalion 507: Commanding officer Hauptmann

Right: A Marder II tank destroyer (Sd.Kfz. 131, a 7.5 cm anti-tank gun on a Panzer II chassis) about to move out.

A Tiger of 2nd Platoon, 1st Company, moving up to its operational area, end 1944.

Schöck, Oberleutnants Koltermann, Küssner and Meissner, Stabsarzt Dr von Malfere.

22 November 1944

Went via Karnievo to 1st Company and reported to its commander, Oberleutnant Beilfuss. He assigned me to 3rd Platoon. Leader 1st Platoon, Leutnant Gerd Eychmüller, Leader 2nd Platoon, Leutnant Heinz Jahn. My crew in Tiger 131 consists of: Unteroffizier Schorling (loader), Obergefreiter Wagner (gunner), Obergefreiter Lukas (driver), Gefreiter Panzer (radio operator). Leo Stückler was appointed loader later. Georg Reinhardt has been promoted to Oberleutnant.

31 December 1944

I have to take on the instruction and general welfare of the Reserve Officer applicants.

1 January 1945

By Volkswagen to 299th Infantry Division and 7th Infantry Division. The major Russian offensive is expected to begin on 11 January 1945. Stabsarzt Dr von Malfere at Mosaki. Drove to 5th Jäger Division and 129th Infantry Division.

13 January 1945

End of peace and quiet.

Anton Seefried

6 January 1945

Went on leave. [His last diary entry.]

There are conflicting opinions as to the fate of Tiger 322: either it fell into Russian hands in January 1945 or was lost in the fighting in the autumn of 1944 to Polish troops in Warsaw. In this photo the track has come free of the drive wheel and the spare track segments on the turret have been dislodged when the panzer was immobilised with explosives by its crew.

Hauptmann Johann Baptist Müller (CO Supply Company): How Did the Ordinary Soldier Live?

Winter clothing with padded jackets and trousers, fur-lined leather boots and hare-fur headwear were excellent. With the aid of the 'Fuchsgeräte' heaters the cooling water for the 12-cylinder petrol engines could be warmed so that even in the worst cold they would start reasonably quickly first time.

Not far from their well-camouflaged Tigers and protected by hedges or similar against snowdrifts, the panzer crews lived in earth bunkers 4 m deep, the roofs being protected against artillery fire by wood beams and earth. These bunkers were relatively spacious, had 'Hindenburg lamps' [tea-light candles] or battery lighting, home-made iron bedframes and a round iron stove to provide a certain degree of comfort. The traditional 'thunderbox' was available for calls of nature and had skilfully designed protection against the wind. At the Vroblev farmstead, the Supply Company quarters about 6 km east of Zichenau, an agricultural leader had previously worked for Gauleiter Koch. This man threshed corn and stocked silos with potatoes and sugar beet well into December and so 507 did not lack for a staple diet.

Johann Baptist Müller: Our Russian *Hiwis*

Many men will remember 'our Russians' who preferred to take their chances with the German Wehrmacht than wait for the Red Army to liberate them from captivity. The Supply Company had about thirty of them whom we put to good use as co-drivers for the ammunition and fuel staffs. They received the same clothing and rations as ourselves and we had the impression that they felt happy to be with us. Shortly before Christmas they asked me if they could attend church in nearby Paluki. My objection that they were not Christians was rejected with indignation as was my objection that they were even less Roman Catholics: 'That is irrelevant. We wish to go.' When I gave in they paraded freshly spruced up, trousers pressed, boots highly polished. After two hours' absence they marched back beaming joyfully and grateful that so much trust had been placed in them,

When I took over the Supply Company, the *Spiess*, Nikolei, suggested as my batman a blond Ukrainian who did not look typically Russian. Nikolei was reliable and always ready to lend a helping hand, but fate did not favour him. In early April 1945 he was at Göttingen station fetching fuel from tanker wagons when USAF bombers appeared and attacked the railway yard. Nikolei ran off to find shelter and on the way was killed by the blast of a near-miss. Honour to his memory!

Johann Baptist Müller: The 1944 Christmas Truce

For many of us it was the sixth time that we had had to celebrate Christmas at the front. Would Ivan ruin it for us? Loud Russian voices through loudspeakers announced a truce: 'We shall let you have your Christmas, but afterwards . . .!' A couple of days before Christmas Eve the lord of the manor at Paulinov invited us to take part in a partridge shoot. He himself brought down a couple of these birds in flight, and we ate them on Christmas Eve. It was already dark

Three crewmen of Tiger 132 near their panzer, end 1944. Note the little roof
against rain above the commander's hatch.

when we were welcomed by the gentleman's very pregnant wife and invited
inside to dine. The room was tastefully furnished with Christmas decorations
and the female Polish cook had prepared the partridge so beautifully that we
truly had a banquet. The war was discussed, of course, and what lay ahead, but
even so the Christmas mood held firm.

Helmut Schneider: A Document of the Time

While Panzer Battalion 507 was resting in East Prussia, it was 'half-term' at
the Officer Cadet Training School, Gross Glienicke, and I had just been made
Fahnenjunker-Feldwebel (officer-cadet sergeant). I was awarded retrospectively
the Panzer Assault Badge Grade 2 and a little later received a small parcel
which apart from cigarettes contained a greetings card from the '*Feldwebeln*
of 3rd Company, Panzer Battalion 507'. I have treasured it to this day.

Kurt Kramer: Advent 1944

In mid-November 1944, 3rd Company settled in at Slasy Slotki, a village
between Mackeim and Karnievo, the other elements of the battalion having

Recovery of Tiger 233. The battalion symbol is visible on the Zimmerit coating.

quarters in the Mosaki area. Still in the shadow of the long arm of the enemy's artillery, we dug in and built some marvellous bunkers. My crew's one even had a white-tiled stove with knee-high surrounding wall. Scarcely had we rested than the military circus began with polishing boots, cleaning weapons, hours of instruction – and the *Spiess* even ventured out on horseback.

Around Christmas the Russian counter-attack was expected from their bridgehead, for our aerial reconnaissance had reported strong enemy forces moving up. Our greatest concern was of being cheated out of our Christmas and so we decided to bring Christmas forward by a fortnight. Ivan had his own calendar!

The village barn was swiftly converted into a ballroom and in dim lighting later even looked like one after inventive minds had provided the decorations. Walter Fuchsig practised his belly-dance for the event. Zinke and Kramer authored a 'Christmas magazine' as ill-begotten as a lurid carnival production. Having neglected to clean the gun of their panzer they were given a dressing-down in the presence of the whole company by the commanding officer who 'could not for the life of him imagine how this lousy crew could ever have the effrontery to present this shitty drainpipe of a gun on parade'.

Nothing could dampen the hilarity of the Christmas event, however, particularly when Claus-Peter Müller unearthed some barrels of pickles in the ground using a mine-detector prod. The truce held and Ivan was even tactful enough to suspend over the Christmas period the regular visits by his Ilyushin 'flying sewing machines'.

About ten days before the real Christmas 3rd Company transferred to the large Helenov agricultural estate north of Mosaki which apparently belonged to Gauleiter Koch. Here there was plenty of room for both men and vehicles and on 24 December 1944, thanks to charitable gifts from the Supply Company and much grog, we celebrated Christmas a second time while teetering on the starting blocks in expectation of the coming offensive.

The 18-tonne tractor has Tiger 233 under tow using metal bars.

'*Big Paw*' – 'The Newspaper of a Viennese Tiger Battalion'.

Heinz Zinke: Toothache During the Lull

We had had a peaceful time in the Karnievo–Mosaki area before being transferred to the advanced lines in mid-November 1944. Our bunkers in the small village of Slasy Slotki had been dug by our predecessors and were now cleaned and enlarged by ourselves. We had therefore become underground dwellers, something which happened only rarely. The front, or in any case our sector, remained relatively quiet except for the usual tension at nightfall when Soviet biplanes which we called '*Rollbahnstenze*' wandered the skies dropping bombs at random. Worst of all was their monotonous engine noise, often of hours' duration, which could be heard whether distant, close by or overhead. When it stopped we knew there was going to be an attack. The pilot would search for the tiniest source of light and then rake it with bullets. I hated these pests with a passion.

Not far from our bunkers were modest huts and large straw-covered buildings like barns. We poor soldiers rummaged through all these structures. What furniture and appointments we found were not worth the trouble of removing them. It was then decided to inspect the earth floor more closely and using the mine-detector probe Stabsfeldwebel Mannsnöther began an intensive search. He was rewarded by discovering that the former occupants of the village had dug deep to store their emergency rations in wooden barrels containing sides of bacon floating in a salty broth. This was very welcome, these being rich in fat. All the floors of all the buildings were eventually dug up and more discoveries made. Some of it tasted of train oil but we didn't complain. The fat in them was the important thing.

The weather was tolerable, the cold not too bad and snowfall modest. Then I developed severe toothache. There was a dentist's surgery, or better said, a portable container of instruments, in the neighbouring village about 3 km away. The way there seemed long, but worse are my memories of the road back. The anaesthetic was a spray. While he was attempting the extraction the tooth broke. The rest was sheer torment. The spray lost its deadening effect (if it had ever had any on the serious inflammation) and the dentist's light to work by was a torch held by another patient. It was already dark by the time the root was removed, which coincided with the arrival of the *Rollbahnstenze* dropping his payload nearby.

More dead than alive I made my way by night through the dark woods, fortunately marked by any number of signposts which enabled me to find my way back and not end up 'on the other side'.

Die Pranke ('Big Paw')

During the rest period at Zichenau–Mielau there appeared for the first time *Die Pranke*, the 'Newspaper of a Viennese Tiger Battalion' edited by the late Leutnant Dr Hans Maul and published in four numbers of which the originals and copies have survived. Issue No. 1 came out on 20 December 1944, the 29th birthday of Hauptmann Fritz Schöck, the CO, who wrote the foreword. Schöck, former Commander of 2nd Company, had taken command of the battalion on 15 August 1944 after Major Erich Schmidt transferred out.

Issue No. 2 appeared on 5 January 1945 and looked at 'The Year 1944 in Retrospect' when our operational areas had been Tarnopol, Brody, Lemberg, Olesko, Suchodole and Kowel. Oberleutnant Max Wirsching was given special mention for having kept open the supply road to Brody while leading elements of 2nd Company. On 20 April 1944 Operation Tarnopol had ended, Oberst Friebe and Major Schmidt had both been awarded the Knight's Cross and the battalion had been moved to the Army Group Centre sector to concentrate its efforts on trying to eliminate the two enemy bridgeheads on the Narew. According to *Die Pranke* during the seventy-seven days of operations the following were destroyed:

Vehicles:	252 tanks,
	80 self-propelled assault guns,
	8 prime movers,
	1 armoured personnel carrier,
	14 towing tractors,
	72 lorries,
	218 horse-drawn wagons.

An unusual recovery procedure in which a Tiger chassis has two other Tigers in tow: end 1944.

Weapons: 74 field guns,
              705 Pak or Flak guns,
              2 automatic guns,
              55 mortars,
              14 heavy MGs,
              135 anti-tank rifles.

Enemy troops: infantry amounting to nine regiments and two companies.

Between 23 March and 17 November 1944 our repair staff and the Workshop Company restored to serviceability 488 panzers and 407 wheeled and half-track vehicles. The achievement of the four repair groups of our fighting companies and Staff Company was quite outstanding. There was almost no day involving our contact with the enemy on which they did not have to go

forward as flying workshops to repair immobilised panzers, exposed on many occasions on the battlefield to enemy artillery and heavy mortar fire and fighter-bombers.

Issue No. 3 of *Die Pranke* appeared on 16 February 1945 and the fourth and last issue on 2 March 1945. Some of the contents can be read later in this chronicle. The editor would like to make today's reader aware that *Die Pranke* appeared in the closing months of the war when the paramount interest was survival. For some

This photo was taken from the rear panzer of the towing group looking ahead to the centre one, turret number possibly 100. Note how the towing cables are attached crosswise.

time the man in the field had not had much enthusiasm left over for 'political tomfoolery' but there was no way he could ignore it. He received regular injections of 'the political picture of the enemy': in reports and orders it was no longer 'the enemy' who was spoken of but 'the Bolshevists', which meant for the common soldier, 'Ivan'.

Here we could insert a long account about the editor of *Die Pranke* of the time, Dr Hans Maul, finding fascination in his appointment as an NSFO (National Socialist Leadership Officer) with the task of instructing members of Panzer Battalion 507 on the 'wealth of National Socialist thinking'. As with all authors, our dear Hans Maul contributes his own experiences in the passages that follow.

One of the last photos of Tiger Battalion 507 in January 1945 during a relief attack. The photo shows Tiger 314 carrying grenadiers on the hull. Subsequently the 507 Battalion personnel retired to Paderborn to reorganise.

Chapter 7

THE FIGHTING BETWEEN THE NAREW AND THE VISTULA

Situation Report

On 12 January 1945 the major Russian offensive began. In our sector, however, it was still quiet. It was known that we had opposing us 2nd Byelorussian Front under Marshal Rokossovski but had no idea of its make-up. As we were to discover later it consisted of 5th Guards Tank Army, 2nd Assault Army, the 47th, 48th, 49th, 65th and 70th Armies, III Guards Cavalry and VII Mechanised Corps, and I and VIII Guards Tank Corps.

The seriousness of our situation announced itself at 0700 hrs on 14 January 1945 with a massive artillery barrage. For us it was a case of warm up the engines, then a short conference headed by the commanding officer in the battalion command post at Mosaki. After this, the companies rolled into the previously ordered operational areas south and south-east of Karnievo as set in preparatory training: 1st and 2nd Companies towards Czarnostov-Szvelice, 3rd Company eastwards towards Slasy Slotki where Infantry Regiment 19 (Regiment List) had already formed a hedgehog from which it would have to be 'hacked free' first.

On this first morning and in the days of battle that followed we soon appreciated that the Russians were carrying out their attacks with a ruthless deployment of men and materials. We also noticed particularly the appearance of massed armour in the form of the heavy Russian JS-2 Josef Stalin tank. Experience of the new Russian tactics was gained on the first morning when 3rd Company Tigers, favoured by mist, approached a large formation of JS-2s to the minimum range of 150 m and destroyed all twenty-two in a brief clash. An undoubted advantage for us was the significantly higher rate of fire of our 8.8 cm gun as against the 12.2 cm gun of the JS-2, which used two-part ammunition. Knowledge of this fact helped alleviate our fear of this new tank from the first day.

Generaloberst Walter Weiss, Commander, Second Army.

Our commanding officer, Hauptmann Schöck, was wounded, though fortunately only lightly, on the opening day of the Russian offensive and so was absent for a few days. During this period the commander of 2nd Company, Oberleutnant Max Wirsching, took command of the battalion, bringing it carefully and successfully through the perils of the next few days.

Now the high morale, excellent fighting spirit and good standard of training of our battalion proved itself and by the end of the second day of combat we had destroyed over 100 of the enemy's tanks and assault guns.

The extract from the *Wehrmacht Bulletin* of 19 January 1945 reads: 'Heavy Panzer Battalion 507 under the leadership of Oberleutnant Wirsching in the Zichenau–Praschnitz area destroyed 136 enemy tanks in three days of heavy fighting. Sixty-six of these victories were achieved in the first two days without loss to ourselves.'

On 27 January 1945 Generaloberst Weiss, Commander, Second Army, mentioned expressly in an Order of the Day 'the steadfast defence of the battalion in the Zichenau–Mielau area where the enemy was forced to halt repeatedly and lost 172 of his tanks'.

Calendar and Diary Entries

14 January 1945 (Sunday)
1st Company (BEILFUSS): Counter-attack south-eastwards Karnievo.

2nd Company (WIRSCHING): Counter-attack south-eastwards Karnievo.

3rd Company (KOLTERMANN): Slasy Slotki.

15 January 1945
Fighting 'eastwards of Karnievo, counter-attack and security north-east Marnostov'.

OBERMAYR: (for A Platoon) Moved to Karnievo.

JÄHN: Commanding officer ordered me to reconnoitre with four selected panzer commanders. We encountered the fiercest Russian defensive fire. In pulling back, my Tiger stuck in a shell crater. Feldwebel Ratayzek pulled us out. We returned with damaged panzers but no casualties. The artillery officer with the CO had his 21 cm mortar battery bombard the Russian assembly area. Feldwebel Klemme, whom I had not taken on the reconnaissance despite his request, fell when hit in the head by a shell splinter.

AICHINGER: Returned from leave. I am with the Supply Company at Vishny. Hauptmann Schöck has a splinter wound to an eye.

16 January 1945
Tank battle at Vielki-Gogole, and at Konarzev. (Unteroffizier Lehmann fell.)

JÄHN: Thirty of our Tigers destroyed seventy Russian tanks, our losses, one.

OBERMAYR: Back to Zichenau.

17 January 1945

JÄHN: Oberleutnant Beilfuss ordered me to take the commander of an infantry regiment to his 'old' command post which, having regard to the way things are, must have been in Russian hands for some time already. Immediately behind a railway underpass we came across a formation of enemy tanks on the move. We destroyed the two leading Josef Stalins and made off.

OBERMAYR: The leader of the Reconnaissance Platoon, Leutnant Moser, has fallen.

18 January 1945

JÄHN: During the night we looked for Feldwebel Behrend in wooded country and in connection with that, led by Oberleutnant Wirsching, brought out the surrounded 'wheeled elements of the battalion'.

19 January 1945

JÄHN: In 1st Company we still have six Tigers operational. The gun of my own Tiger was damaged when a German assault gun reversed into me in a narrow village road. We destroyed three tanks from an enemy column shooting down from a height. At Szrensk we just managed to cross a bridge before it was blown up. The road into Biezun was blocked by a retreating division (probably the *Hermann Göring* Division). I had to perform security for the six operational Tigers. At night I was ordered back to the 'Gut Tepzin' supply base where the lightly wounded CO, back from military hospital, took command of the battalion again.

OBERMAYR: In the early morning arrived at Rippin. Continuing to Strasburg.

20 January 1945

OBERMAYR: Retreating through Goslershausen.

21 January 1945

OBERMAYR: In the morning we arrived at Graudenz.

KÜSSNER: On the retreat to Graudenz the Workshop Company served as a collection point for battalion members without panzers.

The JS-2 tank had the disadvantage that its gun's projectile and cartridge had to be loaded separately, resulting in a slower rate of fire than the Tiger I or Tiger II.

Heinz Zinke:
The Beginning of the Russian Offensive, 14 January 1945

The time passed in endless waiting, roll-calls and cooking until at last on 14 January the Russians unleashed their great Winter Offensive. A carpet bombardment by their artillery covered our entire sector and awoke us early. It was a morning of thick fog. Attack is the best form of defence and so we manned our panzers and advanced into the pea-souper. Warning was given of enemy tanks, but it was some time before we came across them. We halted from time to time to listen, forming up as a company; there was zero visibility and a picture of events was only possible by radio. Our panzer, the 3rd Company command panzer, halted again. The path we had been following had a slight downward slope and then turned left. We could hear the noise of tank tracks

The eclipse of the once so-proud Luftwaffe showed itself in the formation of its own panzer units, equipped with a number of Tigers at the insistence of Hermann Göring. The poster reads: 'Our Luftwaffe. Exemplary fighting spirit and intrepid bravery forged the tradition of the Paratroop-Panzer Division *Hermann Göring*. A special unit of the Luftwaffe, the Reichsmarschall's Division is fully motorised and equipped with multi-purpose and modern weaponry. Young is the Arm, young its spirit, young those who uphold it.'

close by but the enemy was too far away at 50 m to be made out. We stared at the wall of fog in suspense. Suddenly a dark shadow emerged through it. The monster approached astoundingly fast. My first fleeting impression was that it could only be a JS-2 (Josef Stalin) into whose muzzle I was staring. We had the advantage of him, however, therefore AP shell, traverse turret, fire! A hit, knocked out at full speed! The Russian tank came to a standstill, but close behind came a second one of the same type. It approached its stricken partner rapidly, drove around it and then headed for us at maximum speed!

I had it in the sights, hit the trigger, but nothing happened. The commander knocked my knee gently to tell me it was high time to shoot. To my right the loader, also surprised that I had not fired, noticed suddenly that he had not released the safety catch. This lost us precious time. When I brought the second tank to a halt it was literally right in front of us. Why he had not fired was a mystery. At least he could have rammed us, which would certainly have done us no good.

In Memoriam: Kurt Lehmann

On one of the following days, having fallen victim to several mechanical defects, we had gone to an outpost east of Zichenau with six other vehicles. We found cover behind a semi-circle of farmsteads. We had had little rest over the previous few days and could probably have slept standing up. In our command panzer the electrical system was on strike so that neither the intercom nor the starter motor were working properly. Hauptmann Koltermann had therefore transferred to another Tiger, to be replaced by Oberleutnant Heesch as commander. He told me immediately, 'You'll have to handle the fighting, I've got no idea how to go about it.' Despite my objection he then set up the scissors binoculars in the turret in order to be able to follow all that went on.

We agreed that I would advise him 'I am shooting' before firing. We had just refuelled and received our rations when all hell broke loose. Shells exploded all around us. The supply vehicles made off in top gear. We threw everything to hand into the crew compartment, luckily the starter motor worked this time, and we drove to a spot between the houses to 'obtain an overview of the situation'. What we saw through the optics horrified us. Over the broad expanse of lightly snow-covered terrain, almost bereft of any vegetation, about forty Russian tanks of various types were coming for us well spread out and at a good speed. They were shooting as they approached, although the effect of doing this was primarily psychological.

I decided that we had to stop the assault by aimed fire and after the first direct hits had claimed their victims the enemy force turned about to ponder its next move. We remained for hours in our favourable nook and repulsed all further attacks. At midday we withdrew. The ground to our rear was slightly uphill and when we had sight of the summit there suddenly appeared in my sights the protective shield of a large anti-tank gun. Being overtired and unsettled by the constant trickle of attacks, I fired a round at the gun, which passed over it – luckily.

We had reached our main battle line.

We nestled down before our lines on this hill and the infantrymen who had watched our battle from a safe distance were happy to have us as reinforcements. Our panzer stood before the German trenches which had been dug in great haste in an open area. Naturally we did not find this location at all appealing. Our electrical system had meanwhile ceased to function entirely and we could only start the engine manually. Contrary to my advice Oberleutnant Heesch had turned off the engine, and so here we stood.

All was quiet on the enemy side and we could make out no sign of troop movements. But appearances were deceptive. At 1300 hrs on 16 January 1945 – later I saw that my watch had stopped at this hour – we received without any kind of warning a large calibre shell which penetrated the armour near the driver. A host of splinters ripped my padded trousers, another even found my buttocks causing me a major problem later whenever I sat down. My first thought was that this round could be the harbinger of others. The 'scissors binocular' was still mounted in the turret and it took precious seconds for me to convince Oberleutnant Heesch that we had to bale out, '*Raus!*' I demanded several times. Then finally I got through to him and we evacuated the panzer. I rolled over the side of the turret not a moment too soon. Scarcely had I landed than a second shell hit the turret.

Eyewitnesses reported later that this hit released from the turret face a segment of spare track which rose straight up and then fell back between Heesch and myself, striking the Oberleutnant on the head and leaving him with a slight wound. Our panzer was smouldering! Heesch, Kramer, Gamsjäger and I crawled out of the danger zone. Unteroffizier Rolf Meissner's panzer came along and picked us up. That was very brave, for at any moment the enemy could have switched their aim to him.

I was totally done for! Pain in my buttocks and left leg led me to believe I had a serious wound. Fortunately they were only contusions. The several pairs of trousers I wore had taken the brunt of the splinters. Despite the unfavourable position of our wrecked panzer, the radio operator and loader managed to get to our driver, Unteroffizier Kurt Lehmann. He had bolted his hatch and it was not possible to enter the panzer through the hole bored by the shell. Even if he had survived we could not have got him out. Another hit set the panzer on fire. Thus fell in action our comrade Kurt Lehmann, a good and reliable man to us for so long.

Kurt Lehmann was appointed driver of Panzer 331 under the command of Oberfeldwebel Diez when Battalion 507 had been formed. He was the only member of the original crew not to survive the war.

Kurt Kramer: My Last Operational Day in the East

Because 14 January 1945 fell on a Sunday, reveille was set for 0800 hrs, but we were awoken an hour earlier by the Russian artillery barrage. Within a short while we were ready to roll and had orders to advance southwards in order to link up with 2nd Company after crossing a highway. This proved to be impossible because of thick fog. Although 'spreading out' was not feasible for the same reason, we knew the terrain from sandbox games. Instead of 2nd Company, two JS-2 tanks appeared unexpectedly at 50 m range. Zinke neutralised these with two hits to the turret after a ricochet. The fighting around Karnievo lasted three days in all, in the course of which the Russians lost 134 tanks destroyed by our battalion alone. We had hardly any losses, but naturally the usual technical breakdowns.

On 15 and 16 January, 3rd Company was involved in heavy fighting west of Karnievo in the course of which our panzer was damaged and abandoned, and our driver Kurt Lehmann fatally wounded (see report by Zinke above). Although until then we had prevented the breakthrough by the enemy, who apparently had inexhaustible reserves and could bring up streams of reinforcements, the front had to be pulled back eventually because the Russians had broken through on either flank of our sector.

As I remember it was on 17 January close to Zichenau when we ran into another strong tank formation while having only six or seven of our Tigers operational. Towards dusk when we went in search of quarters in a small village and had left our panzers, a great body of Russian tanks, estimated from forty to forty-five, streamed down the opposite slope and headed spread out for our village. Shouts of 'Alarm!' and 'Mount up!' rang out simultaneously. We opened a tremendous cannonade, leaving twenty-five enemy tanks immobile or burning while the survivors fled back up the slope. Unteroffizier Rolf Meissner reported seven kills, ourselves three. I do not remember who else contributed. Apart from a few hits sustained and one breakdown with sprocket damage and brake failure we had no losses. In this case we had had a distinct advantage over the attackers because they had had their work cut out to distinguish between buildings, poultry sheds and so on and our half-hidden panzers.

After the ten-minute-long encounter we took the damaged Tiger in tow and left the inhospitable village. The western horizon was still reddish when we discerned the silhouettes of twelve '*Jupps*' (Josef Stalins) proceeding parallel to us in the same direction.

'We will attack them,' Koltermann said over the intercom. I glanced at the driver. He tapped his temple meaningfully.

Soviet SU-152 self-propelled guns advancing.

I did the same then said, totally without emotion, 'We will not attack them.' It fell deathly quiet above us in the turret. After a while I continued, 'We have only three AP shells left and are towing another panzer.' At that time we did not know that our gun was also damaged after receiving a hit on the cylindrical mantle during the previous action.

Only after a long pause did we hear, 'In order.'

After that we four probably had the feeling that we had dented military discipline but not caused it to collapse: what we had done did not amount to 'forcibly taking over command' or 'cowardly refusal of an order', but had been on the borderline of what was reasonable in the circumstances. Nevertheless I do not hide the fact that I was shitting myself, for it was certain that we would have hardly stood a chance if the order had actually been carried out.

By coincidence, that 17 January 1945 was my last operational day on the Eastern Front. Koltermann gave me the job of using the non-operational

command panzer to tow the damaged Tiger to the workshop at Mielau. The road was lightly rising as we set out, but from its highest point ran straight and much more steeply downhill. The problem was that the Tiger under tow had defective brakes and was therefore not capable of being controlled or steered. Going downhill, no matter what our own speed, it was impossible to prevent the towed panzer catching up. Unrestrained by the towing hawsers it drifted left, uprooted a whole row of trees (with trunks 35cm in diameter) and then came to grief with a violent jolt in a hole 3m deep. The hawser slewed the towing panzer diagonally and stalled its defective engine, and the driver was not able to restart it. While we were deliberating on how to deal with these problems, Hauptmann Steinborn happened to pass by and ordered us to salvage the Tiger in the hole at all costs: he would inform the Recovery Platoon. At that he went back but was not seen again and the Recovery Platoon never came. I dismissed the other crew members with orders that they should break through to the west.

When no tractor had come by next morning, I prepared the demolition charges. In addition to the two Z85 demolition charges which every Tiger carried, we had twelve 1 kg pioneers' charges of dynamite which I considered to be sufficient for the job in hand. It was obvious to me that I had to blow up both panzers together: if I blew up just one, I might not be able to approach the second for the danger of exploding ammunition from the first. The whole business seemed very tricky since after I had set off the first Z85 I would have only 50 seconds to get into the second Tiger and repeat the operation.

I practised a routine: start in the crew compartment of Tiger 1, simulate igniting the first Z85 on the engine hatch, then quickly to the shell rack to do the same thing. Bale out and spring to Tiger 2: grab the antenna, swing over the track guard, jump in, repeat all I had done in Tiger 1, then get out and run for it! I had found a stout spruce tree to give me cover against flying debris: when I reached it I glanced at my watch and groaned: the run had taken well over 60 seconds. I removed my jacket and belt to lower 'wind resistance' and the possibility of snagging on something inside either panzer. After several more trial runs I had it down to almost 50 seconds and decided to chance it. I stuffed my combat pack with three or four salamis which Sepp Placzek had 'organised', two loaves of army bread, an adequate reserve of ammunition for the machine-pistol, and then sat at the edge of the road and waited for whatever would come first, the Recovery Platoon or Ivan.

Using the commander's excellent binoculars I surveyed the area. To the east nothing stirred, although through the trees a village with small houses caught my attention. It was some while before it struck me that these were not houses, since they were moving forward, but Russian tanks, spread out wide and heading westwards at top speed. Now I was forced to act.

Everything went off without a hitch. Scarcely had I reached the spruce tree 20 m away than the first charge went off, but not so loudly as I had expected. The dynamite charge I used on the second Tiger brought about the desired fireworks. The powerful explosion literally tore the panzer apart, causing a hail of steel and wood splinters to whizz past my ears. I was fully protected, however. The force of the blast lifted off the turret and dropped it a few metres nearer me. I buckled up, hung the Leitz binoculars around my neck, put on the rucksack, shouldered the MP 40 and headed for the Reich.

Two weeks later, after playing hide-and-seek with the Red Army, which had meanwhile occupied the territory ahead of me, I saw German soldiers in the distance for the first time. Just east of Graudenz the VW-Kübelwagen of our repairs staff with Oberfeldwebel Hans Strohmeier at the wheel pulled up beside me. He told me that I had been reported missing and brought me to the orderly office where I made my report. Filthy and infested with lice as I was, I asked to see the commander; he was busy with paperwork in an office, heard out the smart recitation of my adventures with little interest, and accepted the return of his binoculars with such a meagre '*Danke schön*' that I was greatly disappointed, although I did recognise that in our present predicament he had no use for binoculars.

Wolf Koltermann was one of the first company members to visit me in my home province of Baden after the war and captivity, and later we met often.

Heinz Stracke: Sand in the Works

During an operation in the Zichenau area, our Tiger had suffered damage to the rear gears, and a new left-side set was fitted in the workshop. On the way to a fresh operation the driver complained constantly of 'oil spraying around his ears'. We called on the repair staff to take a look. Feeling around the drainage tube with a wire brought down oil mixed with sand. The new fitting had been prepared by saboteurs and had to be replaced immediately. This illustrated two important facts: (1) a relatively small amount of damage could limit the mobility of a Tiger and put it out of combat perhaps permanently and (2) the battle-readiness of our fighting companies depended to a large extent on the operational readiness of our repair groups, who very frequently provided their assistance under fire.

Josef Stalin

Naturally not the Bolshevist dictator but the JS-2 heavy tank named after him. The battalion staff issued a dramatic warning one day: 'Stalin tanks in action!' As we were aware, we had to keep these tanks at least 1,000 m away if we were to avoid damage or destruction and injury to personnel. On the other hand, our 8.8 cm gun was only effective against them at a range less than 1,000 m.

About 500–800 m ahead of us we saw a strange-looking bush with something like an oil barrel about halfway up. We let this bush have an HE shell which laid bare a 'Josef Stalin'. Our armour-piercing shell then ended its career.

Johann Baptist Müller: Recollections of a Supply Battalion Commander

Two hours after the Russian offensive began on 14 January 1945, 507 Panzer Battalion was sent into action as virtually the only reserve of Second Army. Deputising for the commanding officer Major Schöck, wounded at the beginning of the offensive, Oberleutnant Max Wirsching, commander of 2nd Company, took command of the battalion. Therefore it was not rank or seniority which decided the substitute by line of succession but experience at the front and proof of worth leading a fighting company.

Towards ten o'clock that night I had gone ahead to Karnievo into the 'hotspot' to reconnoitre and establish the best routes for bringing up supplies of fuel, ammunition and provisions. In the area south-east of Karnievo I met 2nd Company on security watch, well spread out through a sparse wood of pine trees. The panzer men spoke of heavy tank battles all day and into the night in which about seventy Russian tanks had been destroyed for no losses of our own. Other enemy tanks could be seen in the immediate vicinity, and a couple of these monsters could be made out through night glasses. The panzer men were preoccupied by the lack of infantry protection and the fear of Russian close-combat troops. Naturally under these circumstances refuelling and re-ammunitioning was problematic.

Being concerned to maintain full battle readiness of our Tigers, that night I went to the HQ of XXIII Army Corps (Generalleutnant Melzer) in the 'Dominium Opinogora' about 5 km north of Zichenau in order to report on the situation at Karnievo and to request that the corps send infantry support there. Upon conclusion of my detailed statement on the situation as it affected Panzer Battalion 507, General Melzer took my map and with a charcoal pencil drew on it the front line which showed Karnievo as already 'given up'. When I assured him that Karnievo was still in German hands because I had just come from there and seen our Tigers standing security, the general was overjoyed and amended my map in his own hand.

It was 0600 hrs on 15 January when I returned to our panzers to find them still involved in refuelling. Using 20-litre canisters, it took some time to fill up a Tiger whose tank could take 540 litres, and reloading seventy shells was also heavy work. Punctually at 0700 hrs, still not quite light, Ivan resumed his attack. 2nd Company Tigers stood in their loose security line at the edge of woodland. For reasons best known to themselves, the Russians preferred not to enter these woods and chose instead to advance parallel to the edge. This offered the panzers glorious target practice as the Russian tanks passed by. At the end of this second day of the Russian offensive, our battalion could report sixty-six Russian tanks destroyed without loss to itself, a claim given an honourable mention a few days later in the *Wehrmacht Bulletin*.

Dr Hans Maul: The Battle for Karnievo
(from *Die Pranke*, issues 3 and 4)

The battalion had received orders to secure to the south and south-east of Karnievo against advancing enemy tanks. Accordingly 1st and 2nd Companies were deployed towards Szvelice with the command panzer while 3rd Company pushed forward into the woodland south-east of Karnievo towards Slasy Slotki to relieve the command post of Infantry Regiment 19, which had been forced to form a defensive hedgehog.

On this first day of action, only 3rd Company had contact with the enemy. At Slasy Slotki they felt at home by virtue of their knowledge of the terrain, although thick fog limited visibility. 3rd Company Commander Oberleutnant Koltermann could scarcely see his panzers as he gave out orders, mostly leaving the initiative to his platoon leaders.

At 1100 hrs 3rd Company had contact with the enemy when the outlines of five heavy tanks appeared through the mists. These were Josef Stalins with the barrels of their guns pointing upwards and therefore not expecting action. The five colossi were given no warning and short shrift when the range fell to

150 m. Shortly afterwards other enemy tanks appeared and came across the colossi reduced to smoking and fire-spitting ruins. The shock at seeing this caused them to turn off the direction of advance, some milling around wildly amongst themselves and others turning back.

3rd Company naturally used this situation to advantage and Koltermann ordered, 'Bagpipes, give chase and annihilate them!' 3rd Company advanced into the centre of the disorganised mass and by 1330 hrs had destroyed them all. In little more than three hours without loss to themselves 'They destroyed twenty-two Bolshevist tanks turning them into a heap of smouldering metal.' The last of them came to rest before the regimental command post of Infantry Regiment 19, and therefore the task of liberating it had been achieved. Insofar as the situation allowed, there followed the heartiest *'Wiedersehen!'* – our 3rd Company and 1st Battalion, Regiment List, were old acquaintances from the fighting in October for Heights 109 and 107 and the reconquest of Zaklczev.

In the course of the afternoon 3rd Company took up positions ahead of the infantry, but when the fog returned thicker than before, the left wing of the company was detached on security duty to Zelki Dabrove where the Russians were assembling a strong force under the cover of fog.

That same evening Oberleutnant Koltermann learned from the Regiment List command post that the Russians had not expected heavy resistance in this area, and especially not from Tigers. This information had been obtained by our radio surveillance unit listening to the bitter complaint of a Soviet tank group commander that all his tanks had been destroyed by our Tigers.

3rd Company was not engaged in any further tank battles that day but concentrated instead on enemy convoys and the anti-tank guns and the like being brought up.

Whereas the god of war had looked down very kindly on 3rd Company on the first operational day, he seemed not to want to bestow his favour on the other two companies and the fighting staff. In their operational area only a couple of enemy tanks were destroyed. In addition, around 1300 hrs, 2 km south of Karnievo, the commanding officer was wounded under the right eye and had to be taken to the military hospital at Krasne. The wound was fortunately not too serious so that after a few days' treatment he was able to return to the battalion, which had been led in his absence most successfully by Oberleutnant Wirsching.

On the second operational day the battalion was split up: 3rd Company to 299th Infantry Division and 1st Company to Battle Group *Schmidt* of 7th Infantry Division: 2nd Company initially remained at the disposal of the battalion commander. Attached later to 7th Infantry Division, it co-operated with Regiment List as the Russians made their immediate attack on Karnievo.

A Russian T-34 burning after a duel with German panzers.

The main event of this second operational day, especially for 2nd Company, was the bitter fighting around the town. Understandably the Russians had a strong interest in obtaining control of Karnievo as soon as possible because of the Praschnitz–Ostenburg and Mackeim–Golymin–Zichenau road junctions and also the road bridge running through its centre.

2nd Company was south-east of Karnievo with Regiment List and in the early hours had sent a pair of Tigers under Feldwebel Ebner to reconnoitre Zabin-Karnievski and to secure to the south and towards Mackeim. This proved correct for scarcely had the two panzers arrived than a pack of about twenty T-34s and assault guns came rolling up, turned west in front of Zabin and began their push along the road from Mackeim and south of it. This was naturally a piece of cake for Feldwebel Ebner and his companion Scheuerlein, who, in their well-chosen and well-camouflaged positions, simply waited for the unsuspecting enemy tanks to come into range. At optimum range they opened fire and quickly destroyed fourteen of them. The others turned tail and returned to the east.

Despite this first-class victory by the two panzer veterans Ebner and Scheuerlein, a large force of enemy infantry that had been following the tanks infiltrated the eastern part of Zabin-Karnievski and took up positions between the houses. By 0800 hrs Reconnaissance Troop Ebner was back with the company.

The Russians did not allow their plan of attack to be unduly affected by the fiasco at Zabin, and in the course of the morning another strong fleet of tanks forced its way through the Regiment List security line south and east of Karnievo, the overwhelmingly greater strength of the enemy meeting heroic resistance. 2nd Company regrouped to oppose this fresh assault and supported Regiment List. Feldwebel Ebner was now with three other Tigers about 600 m from the north-east entrance to the town. Unfortunately he was unable to prevent a group of three JS-2s and twelve smaller tanks, supported by at least a regiment of infantry, from crossing the road about 1,500 m ahead and pushing on northwards, but otherwise there was a lull here.

At about 1500 hrs a single T-34 came from the east, apparently intending to enter Karnievo, and was destroyed by Ebner at a range of 700 m. Radio surveillance provided the explanation: this tank had made a mistake in the timing and had broken cover too soon. No sooner had we been given notice of this than a group of four JS-2s and four T-34s emerged from the woods south-east of Karnievo and attempted to penetrate the southern part of the town, our own infantry having previously shifted position to the eastern part.

Now the battle for Karnievo began. Almost at the same time as this predicted tank attack materialised, the Russians bombarded the town with murderous artillery and rocket-launcher fire. Shells of all calibres collapsed buildings, causing many fires. The idea was to reduce Karnievo to rubble and so force out the German troops and their commanders. Oberleutnants Wirsching and Reinhardt were surprised in the open as they made their way back to the command panzers from the commander's bunker where they had been making contact with XXIII Corps by telephone. They made it safely through the hail of fire creeping and crawling, suffering no more than bruised knees and elbows. Feldwebel Ebner lost sight of the enemy tank group in the smoke and fumes and when it had cleared the enemy tanks were already in the town to mop up.

Meanwhile darkness had fallen and the German infantry had had to retire to the north, having sustained heavy casualties from the bombardment. The situation for the battalion had become very difficult. 2nd Company and the Battle Staff were north of the town setting up a road block facing oncoming movements from Mackeim. 2nd Company panzer commanders Berthold and Stadler had been cut off from the rest by the enemy panzer wedge recently arrived in the town. There was no chance of resisting the enemy pressure from the south. Wirsching therefore ordered the two stranded panzers to fight their way through to the rest of the Battle Staff.

Enemy tanks and infantry blocked the roads through Karnievo. Besides the usual confusion and chaos of battle, it was a dark winter's night, the roads lit only by the dancing flames from burning houses. The tank obstacles set up by our troops earlier now threatened to become a mousetrap for our own panzers. They had been very speedily mined by the Russians. The gauntlet had to be run. All obstacles were overcome and the two Tigers roared past the Russians, close enough to shake hands. No man or panzer fell into their grasp.

The last of those to break out was Feldwebel Halbritter. In the centre of town his panzer had been attacked by a T-34 which had been skulking behind his quarters. A hit put his intercom and radio equipment out of action. Halbritter had to leave the turret and lie down near the driver's hatch in order to pass instructions to the driver. Then began a race through Karnievo, first a little way towards Golymin, therefore in the wrong direction, then he turned and drove through the formations of enemy tanks and infantry which had assembled in the town centre. Wild shooting came from close range but did no harm and so Halbritter came through successfully.

An equally dangerous but interesting adventure was had by Feldwebel Bloss at the beginning of the tank attack on Karnievo. From the dusk dark shadows suddenly appeared before him identified as KV-85s. One of them drove so close to Bloss that a collision occurred. Bloss had to disentangle his panzer from the enemy, reverse as far back as the closest safe range possible and then fire at the Russian from 20 m. Almost at once he noticed a second KV-85 behind the first, and despatched this one too without resistance. Then Feldwebel Bloss brought his slightly damaged Tiger to the northern exit of Karnievo to join all the others.

The tank barrier erected north of Karnievo meanwhile brought a glorious opportunity to destroy more enemy tanks. From the direction of Mackeim a group of seven tanks and assault guns rolled up in the darkness with their 'rations' loaded on five lorries proceeding between them. As they reached the wreckage of the single T-34 destroyed by Feldwebel Ebner which, still burning brightly, provided good light for shooting, they were as good as done for. The entire column was wiped out beginning with the tail-ender. The flames licking from the wrecks cast a ghostly light on the roads and exit from Karnievo where in November and December of 1944 the men of 2nd Company had spent their off-duty time and visited the cinema.

While it appeared to the battalion commander, Oberleutnant Wirsching, still to be possible to eject the Bolshevists from Karnievo at a single stroke, unfortunately another plan had been developed by the corps command post. Naturally they took great pleasure in receiving our report that on this second day of battle we had destroyed forty-six enemy tanks, but nothing was to be hoped from a planned counter-attack: a new main battle line was already under construction, some of it already occupied by our troops, who had recaptured the territory while Battalion 507 was in action against the Russians 7 km in front of them. Corps therefore ordered that the entire battalion should assemble at Konarzev for re-supply in order to secure and stand ready to repel an enemy counter-attack from the direction of Golymin.

Johann Baptist Müller: Further Observations of a Supply Battalion Commander

Despite our steadfastness, the front line could not be held by panzers alone, and under the pressure of the great numerical superiority of the 2nd Byelorussian Front had to be pulled back to the line Scharfenwiese–Mielau. Although this prepared position was overrun on 18 January by Marshal Rokossovski, our fierce resistance probably convinced him to change his main direction of advance from Graudenz towards Deutsch-Eylau, which fell to him on 22 January. While his army group then headed north to the Frisches Haff on the Baltic, we succeeded, though much disorganised, in reaching the Vistula near Graudenz and assembled there as a company.

At this point mention should be made of the panzer ditches, the building of which had been authorised arbitrarily by the NSDAP Gauleiter Erich Koch without consulting the military authorities defending the 'East Prussian Homeland'. The main panzer ditch ran along the front sector in which 507 Battalion faced the Russian offensive, about 2 km north of Karnievo, towards Vroblev and a little to the south of Zichenau. It did not present the Russians with too much trouble while for 507 it was almost a 'mousetrap' when involved in combat against them or retreating as will be explained in reports later in this chronicle. Some of the crossings or fords had been blown up prematurely by our pioneers which also made things difficult, if not impossible, for us.

Wolf Koltermann: Panzer Battalion 507 in January 1945

We had lost Karnievo and 507 Battalion received the order from corps to assemble the scattered elements in the Konarzev area which, according to Oberleutnant Wirsching, it was still possible to recover. The new main battle line was in the process of being set up at Konarzev and our job there was to secure against anticipated tank attacks coming from Golymin. Since the overall situation had changed drastically and the new front line was being occupied by troops streaming back, the measure was sensible.

The Soviet counterpart to the Tiger II was the heavy Josef Stalin 2 with a 12.2 cm gun. Its successor, the Josef Stalin 3, had not seen action by May 1945.

The political leadership (Gauleiter Koch) was aware of the foregoing and stepped up the excavation work for a panzer and infantry trench system. This was done with little forethought and never in cooperation with the military commanders on the spot or with the higher staffs. The worst damage was wrought in the hectic activity when natural crossings or fords were blown up prematurely, causing serious limitation to panzer mobility: workshop services, supply vehicles and recovery panzers were greatly impeded by these unco-ordinated and irresponsible measures.

Damaged Tigers frequently became write-offs when their destruction became necessary for lack of the possibility of recovery. Despite that, the

Workshop Company and repair service achieved the almost impossible in those January days. The partially delayed and chaotic repatriation of the civilian population to the west is also attributable to the failure of the political leadership. In the course of fighting the retreat we experienced at first hand streams of refugees blocking the roads. Many thousands would have been spared death or martyrdom in fleeing during the icy cold if those responsible had not ignored their duty to humanity. The flight of civilians almost everywhere did not begin until the sound of battle made clear to the population that all promises and solemn declarations by NSDAP district and local group leaders were false and that the Russians were literally at the gates. What chaos, what misery! Naturally our supply vehicles took many of these despairing people back with them insofar as this was possible. They are grim memories which still haunt us decades later, especially those images west of the Vistula when the guarded streams from punishment and special camps were added.

After the loss of Zichenau, our battalion fought a continuous retreat towards Graudenz, alongside elements of 14th Panzer Division that were headed for Schwetz. As a result of technical breakdowns, defects and enemy action, in the last week of January 1945 the fighting section of the battalion reached the Vistula at Graudenz much reduced in size, while the personnel and vehicles of the companies and staffs remained almost intact. Damaged panzers were often brought back into Reich territory for repair with their crews. Therefore it was consistent and logical that the Army High Command should want to transfer Panzer Battalion 507 with its veteran front-experienced crews to the military depot at Sennelager near Paderborn to be re-equipped with the new King Tigers, but extracting it from Second Army presented major difficulties.

Initially all battleworthy Tigers were held at Graudenz with a swollen repairs staff and the battalion's own supply vehicles. Assigned to 1st Company under Oberleutnant Beilfuss, from there they were moved out to Garnsee north-east of Graudenz to help consolidate a planned assembly area. When Marienwerder was declared 'a stronghold' 1st Company was incorporated into its defence and only released when 7th Panzer Division and 28th Jäger Division took over the sector. Reichsführer-SS Himmler had taken command of Army Group Vistula and seized any unit that looked reasonably intact but ultimately the Army High Command order transferring Battalion 507 panzer crews back to Paderborn took precedence.

Chapter 8

THE PARTIAL RETURN TO SENNELAGER

———

Panzer Battalion 507 had been successfully brought together in the Graudenz area. The bridge over the Vistula just north of Graudenz was found intact but did not have the strength to bear the weight of a Tiger. Therefore the last Tigers remained on the east bank of the Vistula with 1st Company under Oberleutnant Beilfuss while the still-battleworthy elements of 2nd and 3rd Companies succeeded in crossing the frozen river to the military depot at Grupe close to Graudenz. The Supply Company was accommodated at a farm at Michelau on the left bank of the Vistula 2 km north of the bridge.

The heavy losses of vehicles suffered by the battalion in the days after the loss of Zichenau were due mainly to technical problems resulting from action with the enemy, or demolition charges. As a result of the serious shortfall in fighting units it became the policy to get badly damaged panzers, or those irreparable locally, back into the Reich proper. Finally 'higher channels' (OKH) ordered the extraction of Panzer Battalion 507 which, as will be explained, turned into a very unpleasant series of events.

On 24 January 1945 at an officers' conference at Graudenz, the first since the Russians launched their major offensive, Reichsführer-SS Himmler announced that he was leading the newly formed Army Group Vistula. In two messages to 507, the new 'Saviour of the Eastern Front' came to our attention by awarding the Knight's Cross to Feldwebel Edmund Rateyczak of our battalion and promoting him to officer with the remark, 'In the Third Reich, achievement is decisive.' This generated the fear that the battalion might be drawn into the defence of Graudenz, now declared 'a fortress'.

As usual our diary entries for the period 20 January to 24 March 1945 (Jähn and Obermayr) are given, together with the experiences of various members of the battalion.

Sennelager north of Paderborn was the formation centre for all Tiger battalions. The photo shows a swearing-in ceremony.

Calendar and Diary Entries

20 January 1945
JÄHN: Tigers into workshop. Commanding officer (Schöck) gave me quarters, a former wheelwright's shop.

21 January 1945
JÄHN: Resting.

22 January 1945
JÄHN: Tigers 102, B and 133 to Rehden. For first time came across columns of refugees. At midnight was ordered to Graudenz military barracks.

23 January 1945
JÄHN: Wrote out recommendations for the Iron Cross.

24 January 1945

JÄHN: Led six Tigers to Garnsee. Feldwebel Rateyczak's Tiger bogged down on sunken road. Secured near railway line. Commanding officer came by at night, ordered that Oberleutnant Beilfuss and Leutnant Jahn take over the panzers while I accompanied the remainder of the battalion to the Reich for rest and reorganisation.

OBERMAYR: Graudenz–Grosswollental.

25 January 1945

HÜLSMANN: Counter-attack towards Unterhenge.

26 January 1945

JÄHN: Commanding officer sent me in the VW to Marienwerder. Crossed the frozen Vistula by night. I have to winkle out the fighting commanders of the Battalion 507 Tigers stationed here. He assures me he will send them off towards Graudenz in the early morning. There is no bridge nearby suitable for a Tiger to cross the Vistula.

27 January 1945

JÄHN: Went with commanding officer to corps at Osterwitt, then to Grupe and 4th Panzer Division at Drez. Our remaining Tigers are being attached to this division, just arrived from Courland. 507's wheeled vehicles are transferring to Grosswollental.

The Tigers from Marienwerder have not arrived! Reichsführer-SS Himmler has been made Commander-in-Chief, Army Group Vistula.

OBERMAYR: Arrived at Grosswollental. The Supply Battery is moving out.

28 January 1945

JÄHN: The transfer to Bütow is beginning.

30 January 1945

JÄHN: Commanding officer and I needed twenty-four hours for the approximately 90-kilometre stretch to Bütow because we picked up refugees on the way.

OBERMAYR: Grosswollental–Preussisch Stargard.

1 February 1945

JÄHN: Drove to 1st Company at Konitz.

OBERMAYR: Arrived at Bütow.

2 February 1945

JÄHN: 1st Company is in action south of Tuchel.

5 February 1945

JÄHN: Looked over printing press of the Büffel Propaganda Company. Telephone conversation with Stettin about train transports

6 to 10 February 1945

JÄHN: Preparations for train transport to Paderborn.

12 February 1945

JÄHN: Train transport of Battalion 507 (less 1st Company) to Paderborn will take until 15 February.

OBERMAYR: 0600 hrs loading at Bütow. Departed 2400 hrs.

13 February 1945

OBERMAYR: Our train passed through Kolberg and Köslin.

16 February 1945

OBERMAYR: Our train stood all day outside Bielefeld. We arrived at Sennelager during the evening.

JÄHN: After arrival at Sennelager camp, until mid-March normal barracks duty with numerous interruptions for air-raid alarms.

27 February 1945

OBERMAYR: Schöck presented Wirsching with the Knight's Cross.

7 March 1945

OBERMAYR: Two *Oberfeldwebeln* of Panzer Battalion 507 have been mentioned in the Roll of Honour. Schöck presented an *Oberfeldwebel* with the German Cross in Gold.

8 March 1945

OBERMAYR: Leutnant Maul went to Berlin to speak with General Ritter von Epp about leave.

11 March 1945

OBERMAYR: Bombers attacked Paderborn.

24 March 1945

OBERMAYR: Koltermann promoted to *Hauptmann* and awarded the Knight's Cross.

Rudi Beilfuss: Madness at the Vistula

The operational elements of my 1st Company remained at Graudenz alongside the reinforced repair staff and our own supply vehicles. After the vanguard of 7th Panzer Division arrived from the east, on 26 January 1945 1st Company was sent north to Marienwerder for incorporation into the defence of the 'stronghold' there. Once 7th Panzer and 28th Jäger Division took over the sector, the wheeled vehicles of 1st Company crossed the ice to the west bank of the Vistula.

The panzers commanded by Leutnant Jahn headed for Graudenz where it was said there was a bridge able to bear a Tiger's weight. This was not only not the case, but the rearward HQ had also not thought of preparing panzer ferries for the Tigers. Since the Russians were now pressing forward to the Vistula, Jahn had no option but to destroy his Tigers with explosives to prevent them falling into enemy hands. In those weeks this was the fate which befell some twenty-two Tigers (though the exact number cannot be confirmed).

For us these proceedings were incomprehensible. What the enemy's 2nd Byelorussian Front had not been able to do was finally done to them by our own side!

Josef Hülsmann (former *Fahnenjunker-Feldwebel*): Tigers at Marienwerder

Four crews were put together from the 'panzer-less' elements of 1st Company and transferred by Leutnant Jahn to Marienwerder. The town had been declared a 'stronghold', and the guns of our Tigers were the only heavy weapons available to the commandant of the fortress. This resulted in our being well fed and supplied, but having to be the 'fire brigade', always on call. Each crew received a bottle of schnapps daily after we informed them that this was the usual practice on active service. The days passed relatively quietly apart from a counter-attack in the direction of Unterhenge on the evening of 25 January 1945 in which we fought a successful duel with Russian

Generaloberst Guderian on a visit to a newly formed Tiger battalion at Paderborn-Sennelager.

anti-tank guns and repulsed the enemy. Our Tigers all received at least some damage and should have gone to the workshop urgently for overhaul. Thus for example, Leutnant Jahn's Tiger went there on the drive wheels because the forward torsion rods had broken.

On 30 January we were released from the 'stronghold' and received orders to proceed to Graudenz in order to cross to the west bank by means of the bridge there. At Marienwerder only the 'ice bridge' had survived. This was naturally not strong enough to take a panzer. The crews were happy to go to Graudenz but then we received Pak fire which put a running wheel out of alignment so that the Tiger concerned had to be destroyed.

A little later we were confronted by an insurmountable difficulty. There was an anti-tank ditch between Marienwerder and Graudenz. The bridge across it had been blown, a fine example of military co-operation. As there were no panzer ferries at Marienwerder, we drove along the ditch in the hope of finding a crossing point, but in vain. The ditch had been created with German thoroughness and actually went up into the Vistula mountains. Therefore we could not get to Graudenz. We had the Russians on three sides and the River Vistula on the fourth, the thickness of its ice not being reliable, and so we had no option but to blow up the three surviving Tigers and then attempt to get to the other side on foot over the ice. Our 'heavily armed group' was equipped with an MG and four machine-pistols and each man had his service pistol. After allowing a strong Russian patrol to pass by below us, we slithered down the slope and made our way across the ice. It cracked open twice under our weight and some open areas could be made out, but finally we arrived unharmed and dry on the western bank where our meeting with the German sentries was a relief from the stress and strain of the last few hours. After that we celebrated our arrival with the Marienwerder schnapps. Next day we succeeded in contacting battalion which sent a lorry to fetch us. Our company commander, Rudi Beilfuss, was happy to have his twenty men back. Leutnant Jahn was court-martialled for blowing up the Tigers but the charges were dropped. I was sent to officer-cadet school at Wischau in mid-March 1945 and therefore took no further part in the operations of the battalion.

Rudi Beilfuss: Odyssey towards Paderborn

The wheeled vehicles of 1st Company reached the old Reich-Strasse 1 at Konitz 4 via Mewe and Preussisch Stargard. The still battleworthy Tigers allocated to 1st Company left Grupe led by Oberleutnant Heesch and fought their way through the Tuchel Heide with other groups. The heavy fighting around Tuchel led to many losses among our operational panzers because the repair staff had no mobile crane and therefore were unable to carry out major works. These locally irreparable panzers were then transported with their crews back to Paderborn where the latter were re-assigned to newly arrived King Tigers or Jagdtiger SP anti-tank guns.

Thus, as of 20 February 1945, only the wheeled section remained behind and finally received permission from Second Army to load up and proceed to Paderborn. Transport was arranged from Berent for 7 March from where the trains headed west via Bütow and Schlawe. Unfortunately at Zanov, Russian spearheads coming up from the south had cut the Danzig–Stettin railway line and the main Stolp–Schlawe–Köslin highway. Our transport returned to Danzig, the assembly point for everything arriving from East Prussia and the cut-off parts of Pomerania.

After occupying quarters temporarily at Neufahrwasser the unit moved on to the port of Gotenhafen. Since these elements of 1st Company had approval to be loaded up, following a request to Army High Command (OKH) by the battalion and after much stubborn resistance, the unit avoided deployment as infantry and all vehicles were loaded aboard a troopship as part of a large convoy which made land seven days later in mist and snow at Swinemünde. From here the vehicles headed at once via Anklam to Märkisch Friedland. Only with a movement order signed by the Reichsführer-SS himself authenticating the Second Army order was it then possible to leave the National Socialist Gau of Pomerania, which had been declared a front region. At Märkisch Friedland the wagons for the onward rail transport to Paderborn were 'procured' and in the last days of March the final stage of this odyssey began.

These remnants of the company were not able to rejoin the battalion at Paderborn, however, and arrived on 6 or 7 April at Bad Lippspringe in the Teutoburger Forest by which time the battalion had to all intents and purposes ceased to exist.

Fritz Schreiber: Remembering my Return to Paderborn

March 1945. Finally the decision had come from Berlin; I was to hand over my repaired Tigers to a 'mixed battalion' which lay ready for action in a village at Frankfurt/Oder. The Tigers were to be loaded at Erkner, which took four days thanks to 'outstanding' organisation. I had obtained quarters with very nice people at Erkner for my crew and myself and from there was able to visit an aunt from whom I obtained assurance that my parents had come through it all and were at Barth, which was a great relief. I handed over my Tigers after we had spent several days in action near Frankfurt/Oder and then we headed back to the old unit at Paderborn.

Because all rail lines to the west had been destroyed we had to try hitching from a couple of stations before Brilon. After much lack of success, Fortune smiled down upon us by 'sending' one of our unit's lorries from Kassel. The diminutive company writer Ansböck thought he was seeing a ghost.

Fritz Schreiber as an *Unteroffizier* and panzer commander, 2nd Company, Panzer Regiment 4, 13th Panzer Division, in August 1942.

Fritz Schreiber in the marshalling yards
at Simferopol station, Crimea.

Fritz Schreiber as a *Feldwebel* with
Panzer Regiment 4.

Fritz Schreiber in the shadow of a Panzer IV chassis, Kuban area, 1943.

Men of the repair staff by a camouflaged Panzer III, summer 1942.

Fritz Schreiber convalescing from
his wound at the Paderborn military
hospital.

Fritz Schreiber's clinical record with
details of the wound received in action
at the Kuban bridgehead, June 1943.

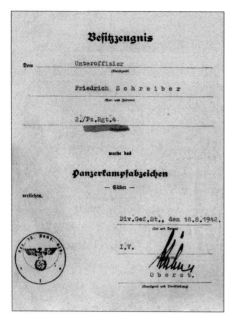

Fritz Schreiber's certificate for the Panzer Assault Badge in Silver, gained while an *Unteroffizier* of 2nd Company, Panzer Regiment 4.

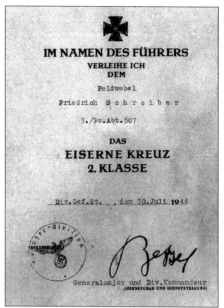

Certificate for the Iron Cross Second Class awarded to Feldwebel Schreiber of Panzer Battalion 507, signed by the division commander General Betzel.

Certificate for the Wound Badge in Silver for three wounds Schreiber sustained on 6 August 1944.

Certificate for the Panzer Assault Badge in Silver, 'for brave participation over 25 operational days'.

'Is it you, *Herr Feldwebel*? We wrote you off long ago!'

Upon arrival at company we had to report first to the *Spiess* for quarters. Even here there was joyful incredulity at the arrival of our missing panzer crew. Naturally it had to be celebrated with a mixture of alcoholic drinks left over from the last 'sergeants' evening'. The motto was, 'Whoever is well lubricated, travels well.' We followed this sensible advice very often.

Johann Baptist Müller: Thanks to Guderian

In the final analysis we owed it to the then Chief of the Army General Staff, Generaloberst Heinz Guderian, for the main body of Panzer Battalion 507 having escaped Himmler's clutches; the first stage of our 'breaking free of the Eastern Front' was the transfer of the wheeled vehicles of all companies (except 1st Company) to Bütow just inside the old Reich frontier.

Johann Baptist Müller: Assembly Point Bütow/Pomerania

In the last days of January 1945, a convoy of wheeled vehicles of 507's Staff Company, the Supply Company, the Workshop Company and the two fighting panzer companies were strung out over several kilometres of the Tuchel heath heading for the town of Bütow about 100 km from Graudenz. Streaming back with us were the endless columns of refugees picked up from villages and farms as we passed.

The main assembly point of the West Prussian trudge was the small town of Berent in the Pommerellen, the coastal region stretching over south-eastern parts of the Baltic. The burgomasters informed us that the columns of refugees would head along the Pomeranian lagoons to the west. The exodus had been fully under way during all January. Whoever saw it will never forget the sight: crying children, pregnant mothers, the hurried covering-over of the recently deceased who could not be buried because the ground was frozen solid. And behind all this misery was the fear of falling into the hands of the Russians.

Mixed into this great withdrawal of the Germans from the east were prisoners of war and the inmates of concentration camps, these latter guarded by SS men. I shall never forget the picture of suffering of a walking 'work column' of female figures, moving along a snow-covered woodland path in the Tuchel Heide in the freezing cold, driven on by their guards like cattle. As I passed by the ghostly column in the staff car, I looked into the many faces close to death and remember seeing bodies here and there in roadside ditches – those who had collapsed and then been given the *coup-de-grâce*, as I observed for myself. This is how war is for those forced to see it.

Paderborn itself was a long-established barracks town.
The photo shows Cavalry Regiment 15 on parade.

Bütow, a small Pomeranian town inside the Reich border, was known for its massive castle which had once housed the Knights of the German Brothers of St Mary at Jerusalem; now it was a haven for refugees of all kinds in those last days of January 1945. There was no possibility of obtaining lodgings: I was overjoyed to be offered an armchair in which to doze at the house of the local midwife. Thousands of refugees from the East Prussian 'Corridor' and the Pommerellen had naturally hoped to get a train west from Bütow, but the railway timetable no longer existed. The Party bigwigs, the 'gold pheasants', had seen to that for 'wheels must roll for Victory' but naturally only eastwards. They fled in their own automobiles when the time came.

The only question for the fleeing masses at Bütow was: how can I get to the west? The word had got round that panzers at Bütow were to be loaded aboard westbound trains. Whilst we waited on edge for the promised transporters, the situation on the Eastern Front had deteriorated dramatically. On 30 January 1945 the Russians had succeeded in establishing bridgeheads on the west bank of the Oder at Küstrin and Frankfurt which meant that the front had advanced 70 km closer to Berlin. Our great concern now was that the Russians might push forward to Stettin/Altdamm and cut the last remaining railway line to the west. Thus it came as a relief when the Reichsbahn notified us that three transport trains would be arriving at Bütow for loading on 12 February.

As our soldiers were well practised in driving vehicles aboard trains, the work proceeded smoothly. In this case, since it was not Tigers which were being loaded but much lighter wheeled or half-tracked vehicles, loading was effected by means of a ramp after the low-loaders had been bridged together with steel plates. This enabled the vehicles to drive up one after the other aboard the forty-seven transporter wagons, then be lashed down and wedged in place once in position.

News of the transporting-out of our battalion had got around quickly and we were hard put to defend ourselves against the throngs of refugees. Under the circumstances who would have refused humanitarian aid? Therefore every free spot, even in the vehicles themselves, was used, provided it was not in the open, for this would have meant certain death in the freezing temperatures.

Our panzer men occupied their vehicles, heated to some extent with the Fuchsgerät engine-warming equipment, the three cattle wagons being given over exclusively to women and children. At the centre of the long train was the field kitchen, richly stocked with provisions of all kinds with hot water always available for beverages. There were no sanitary facilities and the train had to make frequent stops along uninhabited stretches of track. The hurriedly organised system of chamber pots for the children proved insufficient.

Everybody heaved an audible sigh of relief as the train got under way. The route followed was Schlawe–Köslin–Kolberg with a short stop at the latter two stations. Here thousands of refugees stormed the platforms and our trains. It was extremely difficult to get these desperate people to understand that we had only limited ability to accept more passengers: we could only help where it was possible for some to squeeze inside a few of the wheeled vehicles. In order to be able to control the number of passengers I made them all register but unfortunately these listings were lost; they would have been of invaluable help later in enabling families to reunite. Looking back I can say that under the circumstances all went well: there was no illness or accident nor a single case of somebody freezing to death.

The journey continued via Treptow–Gollnow–Altdamm/Stettin. What good luck that the last loophole to the west remained open. Regrettably 1st Company of Panzer Battalion 507, which loaded at Berent on 7 March, found the gates shut.

Upon arrival in Mecklenburg many of our guests left us, including the family of a dentist from Marienwerder (with six pretty daughters) on whose behalf at Bütow we had loaded a large wooden trunk with medical equipment which will no doubt have contributed to the creation of a new life for them.

The efficient eight-wheeled 'Puma' armoured car with a 5 cm gun (Sd.Kfz. 234/2)
was not introduced until 1944 and even then only in small numbers.

The transport steamed day and night via Pasewalk and Neustrelitz. The
general mood relaxed gradually. Our train made an enforced stop at a small
station because of an air-raid alarm and everybody left it for cover. It was
a foretaste of war in the western theatre. On 15 February, after passing
through Wittenberge, Celle and Hannover, we reached our final destination,
Sennelager camp at Paderborn.

Richard Durst: Officers' Celebration in the 'Devil's Mill' Tavern

Our train brought us to Paderborn via Stettin, where we came under MG
fire, and Berlin. At Sennelager camp we were given conversion training to
the Tiger II ('King Tiger'). We NCOs, eighteen or more of us, were given
quarters in one room. In those days there was plenty of booze available from
various sources, pure alcohol and also Guntersblum wine from the vineyard
of our Leutnant Gustl Stadler.

An officers' evening was held in the woodland tavern 'Teufelsmühl'.
Earlier I had had to drive a wood-gas lorry to fetch a group of driver-trainees
so, when I eventually got to the party, most of those present had already

reached their limit, the commanding officer not excepted, for he had had to respond to every toast for his promotion to *Hauptmann* and his Knight's Cross. Once it ended I had to load as many 'bodies' as possible in the back of the lorry. An *Oberfeldwebel*, possibly Fritz Breitfeld, accompanied me as co-driver, which was just as well since driver and passengers were far from sober. We crossed the airfield towards Sennelager, arriving there safely even if some of the passengers had nasty bruises to show for it.

This photo shows the later Generaloberst Guderian as an active commander at the front in his command vehicle (Sd.Kfz. 250/3) in 1940–1. From 1 March 1943, as Inspector of Panzer Troops, he was responsible for the modernisation of motorised sections of the Wehrmacht and worked in close cooperation with Albert Speer on the development of new panzer designs.

Chapter 9

THE BATTLE OF PADERBORN

By March 1945, the Allied armies had made such deep incursions into Germany that the Reich had been reduced to the territory between the Rivers Oder and Rhine. In the West, the Americans and British were anxious to close the Ruhr Pocket and seize Paderborn for its panzer centre at Sennelager.

2nd and 3rd Companies of Panzer Battalion 507 (as has been noted, 1st Company was still involved in an odyssey which would result in it never arriving) were involved in converting to the Tiger II. This required a re-training of crews, new supply vehicles, particularly vehicles and equipment for the repair services, and this was by no means complete when it became necessary to deploy Panzer Battalion 507 against the US Army on the Rhine-Westphalian defensive front as part of a Waffen-SS panzer brigade.

In 1982 I started compiling a file of experience reports on the Battle of Paderborn which occurred at Easter 1945, and in 1985, forty years after the event, I brought these files to the attention of the British Training Centre for Staff Officers. I received an invitation from them to visit Paderborn for the fortieth anniversary celebrations. The details I supplied in my report regarding movements, times and incidents involving the battalion were checked over during the 'Battlefield Tour' of the British Army of the Rhine from Sennelager on 27 and 28 March 1985. My report can be considered objective to a considerable extent, while contemporary German academic literature (Dr Hohmann and Willi Mues) and also the reports and interviews with former officers of 3rd US Armored Division 'Spearhead' were subjected to the same scrutiny (*Editor*).

Calendar and Diary Entries

27 March 1945

OBERMAYR: Heavy bombing raid on Paderborn. Drove in the evening to help in the clear-up.

JÄHN: Major air attack on Paderborn which I experienced in the public air-raid shelter under the post office. Operation to rescue many civilians from the burning buildings. My motorcycle and sidecar buried under the rubble. At night I reported to the commanding officer. The battalion is on the outskirts of town and could not get to the town centre because of the debris in the streets, and neither could the numerous fire brigades arriving from surrounding towns.

Panzer wrecks can be seen in nearly all photos of 507 Battalion Tigers after the reorganisation at Paderborn in 1945. Most of these photos come from US military sources. This American soldier is seen posing in front of an immobilised Tiger II with the turret number 121.

Wolf Koltermann and Fritz Schreiber:
Action Involving 3rd Company, 30 March 1945, Paderborn

On 28 March 1945 Panzer Battalion 507 was still in the process of conversion to the new panzers, of which 3rd Company received all fifteen 'thoroughbred' Tiger IIs delivered. These still had to be run-in and the weapons calibrated. After the crossing of the Rhine at Remagen, the enemy's turn north at Marburg pointed to Paderborn as the next objective for the US divisions – later confirmed by our own reconnaissance. As a result SS Panzer Brigade *Westfalen* was formed during the hectic activity of those days and hours. Placed under the command of SS-Obersturmbannführer [Lieutenant-Colonel] Hans Stern, its purpose was to defend the military district on the flank south of Paderborn. The brigade was hastily assembled, mainly from Waffen-SS panzer units under training at Sennelager, and Panzer Battalion 507 was the only Army panzer element attached. On 29 March an alarm of twenty-four hours' notice was given to move out battle-ready.

Major Schöck remained our commanding officer, having led the battalion since the summer of 1944 with extraordinary success. 1st Company, with its main force under the command of Hauptmann Beilfuss, was eventually unable to rejoin the remnants of the battalion until April. The commander of 2nd Company, Hauptmann Wirsching, had been transferred out to command a battalion of heavy anti-tank Jadgtigers. This had led to a number of changes in the platoon leader and panzer commander structures of the companies.

At 1030 hrs on the morning of 30 March, the battalion left Sennelager and headed for the assigned assembly area, the woods at Dahl–Dörenhagen–Eggeringhausen. Because the streets of Paderborn remained impassable for traffic, the route followed by the armoured column was the bypass road to the south-east of Paderborn (the modern B68), a distance of about 10 km. Meanwhile, 10 km south of Paderborn, the towns of Nordborchen and Kirchborchen had become the scene of heavy fighting between SS Regiment *Meyer* and US armoured forces.

At 1300 hrs, at this time 2 km from Dörenhagen and therefore still short of the assembly area, 3rd Company received an order from Major Schöck to divert to Eggeringhausen and, 'being at readiness to engage the enemy', there turn west and head along the road towards Kirchborchen 'to relieve SS Regiment *Meyer* and block the enemy tank advance to Paderborn'. Careful reconnaissance was an absolute necessity.

At about 1430 hrs 3rd Company reached the Eggeringhausen–Kirchborchen road. It was necessary here to proceed in single file because of the dense woodlands on either side. Anti-aircraft machine guns were manned

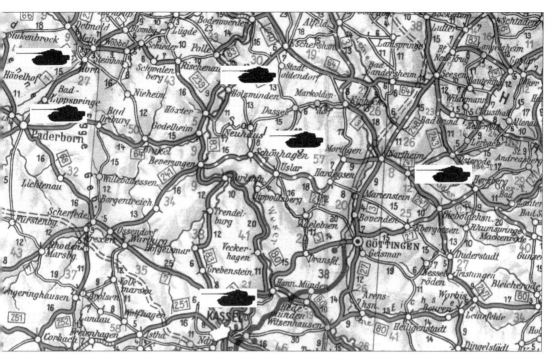

Map of the Paderborn area eastwards to Holzminden and Osterode in the last
month of the war. At the foot of the map is the town of Kassel, home of the
Henschel factory where Tiger Is and IIs were completed.

and ready. After a kilometre the undulating countryside on both sides of
the road opened out up to 500 m and therefore became 'panzer-capable'.
3rd Company proceeded in stages in a broad wedge formation from hilltop
to hilltop, Hauptmann Koltermann and radio operator Kurt Kramer going
ahead on foot each time to view the next sector of terrain.

After another 2.5 km of cautious approach the terrain opened out wider
from the Hamborn crossroads. Beyond lay the slope rising to the Kühlenberg
about 800 m farther west. The foot reconnaissance showed that Kirchborchen
was held by the Americans while Nordborchen, closer to Paderborn, was now
apparently at the heart of the fighting. At its eastern side a strong security line
of tanks, if not an assembly area, could be made out. Our every movement
on a hilltop came under immediate aimed fire from tanks or anti-tank guns.

At 1515 hrs Koltermann had his three platoons advance to positions on the
reverse slope of the arid Kühlenberg elevation, two to the south side of the road,
one to the north side. The range to Nordborchen was about 1,000 m, visibility
relatively good, and we opened fire on identified, especially armoured, targets.
A number of tanks and a series of tracked or wheeled vehicles were put out of

action. Movement in the villages ceased at once, and soon we received heavy artillery fire on our position which we countered by frequent shifts of location. We suffered no losses.

Our appearance at Borchen and opening fire on them apparently unsettled the Americans, for after 1600 hrs we came under attack from low-flying fighter-bombers strafing us with their cannon and dropping HE and phosphorous bombs. They were so skilled at low-level flight as to instil anxiety and fear in us, and they were not intimidated by the machine guns mounted on our panzers. It is difficult to describe the feeling one had watching their bombs falling, the craters they made being large enough to take three panzers! Often we disappeared in great clods of earth, fumes and fire, many panzers over 60 tonnes in weight jumping about! However many panzers these *Jabos* might have claimed as destroyed upon returning to their airfields is not known, but only one panzer received a direct hit from a phosphorous bomb; it slid off the sloped front armour and thus did no damage. Meanwhile, an enemy armoured unit was attempting to go around us, the intention being obvious and this was reported at once by radio.

From our first experience of battle against American attack formations, we established that their 'spearheads' held back at once upon encountering serious resistance, sent up their aerial spotters and used well-directed artillery fire to clear the path of their advance from any obstruction. At this time of course our own forces no longer had any aerial nor artillery support. We also had the additional considerable handicap of no repair workshop so that almost every technical defect or item of damage led to the panzer having to be written off. After 1700 hrs, or in any case about half an hour after the departure of the last *Jabo* and the resumption of our shooting at targets in Nordborchen, we received warning from Major Schöck at Staff HQ that an enemy armoured column advancing from the south had come under fire from the security platoon commanded by Oberleutnant Jähn at Dörenhagen/Eggeringhausen. It had been forced away but, undeterred, the enemy column was now approaching our rear along the same Eggeringhausen–Kirchborchen road as we had used to get to where we were. Koltermann's orders were to allow the enemy armour to come up and then wipe it out: we were free to act as the situation dictated, and constant radio readiness was agreed upon.

Top left: Tiger 402 abandoned in front of an inn in Dörgestrasse, Osterode.
Left: Detail of the turret of Tiger II 402. An American photographer is pointing at a hit by an armour-piercing shell. Note the towing loops and the two-part spare track segments.

At dusk, towards 1800 hrs, the company commander issued his preparatory orders for battle:

'Immediate radio readiness for the whole company. Extreme radio discipline. Position "301" [command panzer] continues behind crest of road.' Then, acting one after the other, 1st and 3rd Platoons were to about-turn and remain on the slope to face the approaching armoured column:

'2nd Platoon, formerly positioned close to the south side of road, will leave it in individual units while maintaining an intensive directed fire from either side of the road so as to deceive the enemy as to our regrouping.

'As soon as that is effected, 1st Platoon, formerly on the southern flank of the company, will withdraw in individual units, take up position north of the road and face east. Direction of fire is the edge of woods, 700–800 m range, field of fire allotted, south of the road (to the right), where it leaves the woods.

Side view of Tiger 402 with turret facing to 'six o'clock'. The position of the turret was changed frequently.

Tiger 402 was towed from Dörgestrasse to the Königsplatz at Osterode
where it remained for some time.

'As soon as that is effected, 3rd Platoon, formerly on north side of road, right flank of company, will, after 1st Platoon has concluded its movement, also fall back, face east and assume the most favourable firing position facing edge of the woods north (left side) of the road to where the reported enemy force must come.

'Careful measurement of range by commanders. Load AP shells, weapon at readiness to fire. Otherwise everything as per 1st Platoon. Both 1st and 3rd Platoons must allocate the outer panzer to secure the flank. Open fire, if at all possible, as a sudden surprise concentration of fire but only on the order of the company commander.'

The re-grouping of the company was completed shortly before 1900 hrs practically in twilight. By then the crews had familiarised themselves with the terrain in front of the woods. A little later the enemy could be heard approaching, almost textbook style. A reconnaissance tank drew up on the road about 100 m before the edge of the woods, stopped briefly and then had fifteen to twenty tanks come forward and form up at once on both sides of the road in a kind of wedge formation. Hauptmann Koltermann then ordered recognised enemy tank targets to be taken under fire, and within a few minutes nearly all the tanks of the first wave, served up on a platter, were ablaze, and also the tanks and other tracked armoured vehicles following behind from out of the woods.

The impression we all gained in the brief half-hour of the first battle phase was that the Americans had failed to spot our two platoons on the forward slope, and because of the heavy firing towards Kirchborchen and Nordborchen by 2nd Platoon they had assumed it was safe to make an attack into our rear. Up to that point we had no casualties or serious damage to vehicles.

Eventually Tiger 402 was towed from the Königsplatz at Osterode over the Dielenplan to the Söse Promenade, providing the townspeople with a minor attraction on the way.

Tiger 402 was finally scrapped on the Söse Promenade at Osterode.
The number can just be made out on the side of the turret.

We had not been provided with details of the American battle group's strength and composition when the warning had been given and it was impossible to make any useful assessment from the confusion of burning and wildly manoeuvring enemy vehicles at the edge of the woods. Since the enemy force had no effective leadership, at 1930 hrs Hauptmann Koltermann sent a situation report to Company HQ and requested permission to attack. On the condition that the security platoon covering Borchen remained in position, limited consent was given to proceed as far as the edges of the woodland.

The woods were 250 m away and allowed the two platoons to spread out. At 1945 hrs the company received radioed orders: '2nd Platoon will remain in the present positions with previous objective. At all costs maintain radio watch. Further orders follow. 1st and 3rd Platoons will proceed immediately and wipe out enemy totally, making short stops to fire during the advance. Be economic with AP shells! Guard your flanks!'

With the so-familiar order 'Panzers roll!' a period of night fighting commenced which was to last for two hours. From the outset we moved ahead only slowly because of the need for some 'clearing up' to be done in the forward battle area. The surviving crew members of the wrecked twenty-four

Captured German officers at Osterode answering questions about the Tiger.

tanks and armoured vehicles – some of them still burning – had made off into the woods on the far side and now it was left to us to destroy the non-burning vehicles by gunfire at close range. Even the last tank which had hoped to escape detection behind a barn was spotted.

Kurt Kramer: The Breitfeld Barn

The story of a tank which had hoped to find cover behind a barn was probably repeated a thousand times over during the war. The following anecdote demonstrates how a lonely barn on the Eggeringhausen–Kirchborchen road came to lend its name to the incident.

View from the turret over the long 8.8 cm gun of a Tiger II.

This Tiger II of Heavy Panzer Battalion 508 came to a halt for lack of fuel at Polle on 8 April 1945 and was abandoned.

In 1985, during a battlefield tour with British and US officers, we stood on the same high ground, the so-called 'Kühlenberg', from where forty years previously two platoons of our 3rd Company had delivered a severe defeat to our American opponents. None of the topography had changed since then: before us the slightly sloping terrain, devoid of vegetation to the edge of the woods 800–1,000 m distant, and halfway there, alongside the road running through the terrain an 18 m long stone-built barn.

Sheltering behind this barn had been an American tank, probably the last one still mobile and capable of resisting. Up to this point the battle had been little more than shooting down from a bare hillside, but in this second phase it had moved towards the woods. The 'hidden Sherman' presented us with a serious danger.

Until then I had been busy with my double-function radio equipment and had had no time to watch what was going on outside the panzer. I received a radio message from Oberfeldwebel Fritz Breitfeld. He requested permission to search out the Sherman. Hauptmann Woltermann approved after some consideration, but added a warning to exercise the greatest caution. But what did this word 'caution' mean? The Sherman would fire first if his gun was pointing in the direction from which Breitfeld would appear. It was a game of poker, but actually the risk was much greater, for other enemy tanks might suddenly appear from the woods only 500 m away.

The tension amongst the spectators 'on the open stage' was indescribable. Breitfeld's King Tiger made a halt 30 m short of the barn as if he were not sure whether to go left or right of it. Then everything happened at once. The turret traversed to nine o'clock, the panzer moved forward to the right of the barn, stopped, and a split-second later the 88 fired. The explosion behind the barn, the cloud of smoke soon rising above its roof, showed that the Sherman had come off worse in the duel!

Between the Caucasus and Paderborn I cannot ever remember having seen a more courageous individual action. There must have been many such, especially when only the T-34 was really equal to the 88. For a King Tiger versus a Sherman, the chances were distributed rather differently. Breitfeld survived the war but was unable to attend our reunions until the Berlin Wall came down.

Wolf Koltermann and Fritz Schreiber: More on the Good Friday Battle

The infantry response which flared up occasionally from the edges of the wood was ineffective but showed us which side required our closest attention. In the long stretches of glades total chaos reigned. The road was almost completely blocked by tanks, command and supply vehicles strewn at all angles or crashed together and here too most of the crews had fled into the woods or driven off the road at our approach. In this phase of the battle we encountered resistance which flared up repeatedly, enemy soldiers putting up a bitter fight with hand-grenades and machine pistols. Wheeled vehicles which had been abandoned were pushed aside by our panzers. This economised on ammunition! Apart from a jeep acquired by the company commander, the important acquisitions were American battle rations and packs of cigarettes.

At 2100 hrs 2nd Platoon covering Nordborchen had reported itself out of ammunition and requested further orders. The firing here had almost ceased. For 1st and 3rd Platoons the situation as regards ammunition was similar and Woltermann asked Company HQ for re-supply and new orders since the objective had been more or less achieved and it was not advisable to remain.

Right: This Tiger II (obviously seen here after the end of the war) was attached to 507 Battalion but the location has not been identified.

Despite artillery fire, fighter-bomber attacks and several contacts with mixed enemy armoured columns coming up from the south, the territory and roads leading to Paderborn and Hamborn were under our control.

At 2200 hrs Major Schöck ordered: 'The platoon masking Nordborchen can be withdrawn to rejoin the 1st and 3rd Platoons and after completing their purpose in securing and cleansing area will retire to Eggeringhausen (forest lodge).' It was in the hour after 2200 hrs that the controversial incident occurred in which Major General Maurice Rose was shot dead while attempting to surrender.[1]

The 'ploughing over' of the sector, confirming that all enemy vehicles had been permanently disabled and that the shooting from the edges of the wood had been silenced, terminated at 2245 hrs. From the count of heads we had suffered no casualties. In the report of the enemy vehicles destroyed only the twenty-four armoured vehicles (tanks, assault guns and armoured personnel carriers) from the first phase were counted while the remainder were classified as 'the column of wheeled and half-track vehicles belonging to them'.

After being stood down from battle readiness, at 2300 hrs the company formed up in file and headed for the woods around the Eggeringhausen forest lodge. The company commander led the way in the captured jeep with an American staff officer as prisoner to be handed over to our staff. This officer made great efforts to persuade us 'to abandon the struggle' and made an outstanding impression but his name cannot be recalled.

Just before Eggeringhausen the command panzer 301 came under fire at very close range. The thick armour absorbed the hit, the 'dent' being deep enough to accommodate two fists. The round was fired by a panzer of the 2nd Company security platoon under Oberleutnant Jähn who had not been advised of events and had assumed that a column of tanks led by a crowded jeep must be American! We reported back to the commanding officer at midnight bringing the eventful day to an end.

---

1.   Rose and his command party, travelling by jeep, blundered right into a group of King Tigers. Obviously outgunned, and with no chance to escape, they had no option but to surrender. Rose was trying to unbuckle his holster to give up his pistol but was shot because one of the Germans thought he was attempting to use his weapon. No charges were brought subsequently.

A Tiger II alongside the wall of the convent at Wiebrechtshausen.

Kurt Kramer: Paderborn 1945 – A Reflection

Paderborn was for many wartime participants a kind of 'home town' for many branches of service but especially for panzer troops. At the outbreak of war it had been the depot for Panzer Regiment 11 with its reserve and training battalions. Later it became the 'cradle of the Tiger battalions'. The men of 507 received their training here and after almost exactly twelve months, in which they came through numerous battles on the Eastern Front, they returned here for reorganisation, followed by battle in the new King Tigers against the US Army. This extremely successful action was also the last in which 507 was active on any large scale. We learn of this from diary entries

and essays recounting experiences by Feldwebel Fritz Schreiber (Tiger II commander with 3rd Company), and Hauptmann Wolf Koltermann (Commander, 3rd Company) as well as another participant of the times Oberleutnant Dieter Jähn (Platoon Leader, 2nd Company).

Today one can debate what were the most important reasons for our success on 30 March 1945. Was it the tactically correct decisions made by our commanders, the battle experience of the panzer crews or the superior armour and armament? Certainly these were important factors, but as we may view it today, an important role was played by good luck and the gross tactical lapses of our opponents then (3rd US Armored Division 'Spearhead'). Officers of this US division stated at a meeting in Paderborn in 1985 rather reproachfully to participants of our unit that our success was only achieved 'by luring Battle Group Welborn into an ambush'.

Even if being 'positioned on the slope of a hill devoid of vegetation' can be described as an ambush, in wartime an ambush is not illegal but a skilful tactic. On the evidence presented, it is more correct to say that we had prepared for a situation caused by a lack of reconnaissance and communication by the enemy units, especially since we had been the target for fighter-bomber attacks and artillery fire on our position on the Kühlenberg. It remains a mystery why Battle Group Welborn chose this fatal road westwards and thus fell into a trap of its own making after coming under fire from the rearward security platoon commanded by Oberleutnant Jähn of 2nd Company.

The Battle of Paderborn had no real influence on the war. The closure of the Ruhr industrialised area to the west left open to us only retreat eastwards. From this time onward there were no more co-ordinated, tactically planned and executed operations but rather only fragmentary actions, one Tiger after another becoming disabled through technical defects.

Calendar – Extracts from Oberleutnant Jähn's Diary

31 March 1945

The attempt to recover two damaged Tigers cost us the loss of two towing vehicles to enemy fire. This afternoon about twenty-five Shermans advanced along the Paderborn–Kassel road near Eggeringhausen. Unaware of US tactics and morale we opened fire too soon. We destroyed five enemy tanks (gunner Unteroffizier Fedderke); the other twenty withdrew. After that we received heavy artillery fire. We were forced to change position, lightly damaged in transit, but sustained no personnel casualties.

1 April 1945

Very heavy artillery fire without pause. We fetched fuel from Heuenheerse.

2 April 1945

In the early hours (still dark!), advanced to Willebadessen where the Americans were sitting in their tanks. Up to village entrance no contact with enemy. Before the SS infantry support arrived we came under fire from well-camouflaged tanks and anti-tank guns. My Tiger was put out of action. The operation cost us five Tigers while we destroyed five of their tanks and additionally others with Panzerfausts. We consider it a failure, however. I received splinters in the forehead and lower right arm and was taken to Bad Driberg military hospital.

American troops at Ottbergen posing by the wreck of a burnt-out Tiger II. The track on the road was shed by a Panther.

Another wrecked 507 Battalion Tiger II at the Wiebrechtshausen convent. Tiger wrecks were popular subjects for photography by American troops.

OBERMAYR: 0200 hrs. Advance with Waffen-SS to Willebadessen. In the village we had five Tigers destroyed, all SS officers were wounded. Also Novotny dead, Leutnant Eckart wounded.

4 April 1945
Am informed that 1st Company unloaded at Hamelin after a true odyssey.

8 April 1945
I reported back to commanding officer, Major Fritz Schöck, at Moringen.

10 April 1945

Went to C-in-C Panzer Troops (West). In the afternoon with repair unit destroyed four enemy tanks with Panzerfausts.

11 April 1945

East of Northeim, tank battle near forest. Moved over to Osterode. Heavy artillery fire. Our panzers have been released to an SS unit.

Rudi Beilfuss, 1st Company

After returning to Germany on 4 April at the end of our odyssey, we were required to pass our panzers to an SS unit and continue by wheeled vehicles to Magdeburg where new panzers would be waiting for us at 'Army Wenck' for the defence of Berlin. At Magdeburg we discovered that the panzers had been passed to another unit and OKH at Zossen was at a loss as to what we should do next.

Kurt Kramer: Our Last Tiger

About 11 April 1945 our last Tiger came to a stop with an irreparably damaged engine after crossing a bridge into the small village of Freiheit near Osterode (Harz). Its commander, Unteroffizier Claus-Peter Müller, was given orders to defend the panzer to the last by keeping its turret aimed at 'six o'clock'. I volunteered to deliver rations to the crew and when I arrived I found that he had concluded a 'separate peace' with the Americans and was living with his crew in comfortable lodgings nearby with a 'Damenquartette'.

Everybody knew at this point that the war was lost.

The aerial bombing of German cities and towns intensified from 1943 onwards. Here the French cathedral in Berlin blazes like an enormous torch.

Panzer-grenadiers were often dropped off and left to their own devices: the Panzerschreck, or 'Stovepipe' (*left*), and Panzerfaust were Germany's standard infantry anti-tank weapons.

This well-camouflaged Tiger II, seen at Uslar on 8 April 1945, was attached to Panzer Battalion 507.

This 507 Battalion Tiger II ended its career in front of the Klosterkrug restaurant at Falkenhagen. It came from one of the first series of fifty to be built, identified by its rounded Porsche turret.

Opposite, top: An American bulldozer attempting to push a stranded Tiger II off the road into a ditch: photo taken at Hartes on 9 April 1945.

Opposite, below: German soldiers surrendering their weapons to an American unit.

German troops in a north Italian town marching into Allied custody.

German prisoners of war returning home after a long spell in captivity
in the Soviet Union.

CONTRIBUTORS

This listing includes (where known) each man's full name and final rank along with a note on their role within the battalion and the nature of the material they supplied during the making of this book.

Aichinger, Unteroffizier Erwin: HQ Company. Diary.

Beck, Siegfried (rank unknown): driver, Tiger 311. Diary and experience report.

Beilfuss, Hauptmann Rudi: leader 1st Platoon, 1st Company. Experience report.

Diez, Oberfeldwebel Heinrich (later Leutnant in another unit). Diary and experience report.

Durst, Unteroffizier Richard: Repairs Staff, 3rd Company. Diary and experience report.

Eychmüller, Leutnant Gerhard: platoon leader, 1st Company. Diary and experience report.

Gebhardt, (Officer cadet)/Oberfeldwebel Rolf: Knight's Cross; platoon leader, 2nd Company. Herr Thomas Leim supplied photos from his collection and photocopies of his award certificates.

Gutmann, Helmut (rank unknown): panzer driver, 2nd Company. Diary.

Hagenberger, Gefreiter Hubert: panzer driver, 3rd Company. Diary and experience report.

Hülsmann, (Officer cadet)/Feldwebel Josef: 1st Company. Experience report.

Hüpfl, Unteroffizier Sebastian: gunner, Tiger 201. Note about his wounding and hospitalisation.

Jähn, Leutnant Dieter: platoon leader, 1st Company. Diary.

Jahn, Oberleutnant Heinz: 2nd Company. Diary.

Koltermann, Hauptmann Wolfgang: Knight's Cross; commander, 3rd Company. Situation and experience reports.

Kramer, Unteroffizier Kurt: radio operator, commander Tiger 300. Experience report.

Küssner, Oberleutnant (Ing.) Helmut: commander, Workshop Company. Experience report and correspondence; Frau Barbara Scharf, his daughter, supplied photographs.

Maul, Leutnant Hans: commander, Tiger 323; staff officer, HQ Company. Edited regimental newspaper *Die Pranke*. Original editor-in-chief of 507 Chronicle.

Müller, Hauptmann Johann Baptist: commander, Supply Company. Experience report.

Obermayr, Siegfried (rank unknown): Reconnaissance Platoon. Diary.

Raab, Obergefreiter Franz: panzer driver, 3rd Company. Diary.

Seefried, Anton: Oberschütze. Reconnaissance Platoon, 3rd Company. Diary and experience report.

Scheuerlein, Feldwebel Ludwig: panzer commander, 2nd Company. His son Ludwig provided photographs.

Schneider, Leutnant Helmut: commander, 1st Company. Later editor, situation and experience reports, photos and diary extracts.

Schöck, Major Fritz: Knight's Cross; last commander, 507 Btn.; photo supplied by Frau Gabriele Steinbrick and Herr Rainer Michael Schöck.

Schreiber, Feldwebel Fritz: panzer commander, 3rd Company. Supplied photos from his personal collection.

Steinborn, Hauptmann (Ing.) Johann: Workshop Company. Letter.

Stracke, Gefreiter Heinz: radio operator, 3rd Company. Experience report.

Wirsching, Hauptmann Maximilian: Knight's Cross; commander, 2nd Company. Experience report.

Zinke, Unteroffizier Heinz: gunner and commander, Tiger 300. Experience report.